THE WIND A'ı ᴍʏ ʙᴀᴄᴋ

VICTOR ECHEVARRI WALDRON

MINERVA PRESS
MONTREUX   LONDON   WASHINGTON

THE WIND AT MY BACK
Copyright © V.E. Waldron 1996

ISBN 1 85863 733 3

First published 1996 by
MINERVA PRESS
195 Knightsbridge,
London SW7 1RE

Printed in Great Britain by
B.W.D. Ltd., Northolt, Middlesex.

THE WIND AT MY BACK

This book is dedicated to my wife Olivia, who supported me in writing it, helped me shape it, co-lived so much of it, that without her, it would not exist.

After World War II service in the British Royal Navy, his career covered six years in politics, as a member of the Conservative Central Board of Finance, a parliamentary candidate, and Financial Advisor to the Constituencies. He is now retired from business where he held a number of directorships. Today he is a member of the Foreign Press Association of London, the Overseas Press Club in New York and of the Diplomatic & Commonwealth Writer's Guild in the United Kingdom.

He is an active Campaigner against World Hunger and a supporter of the English Speaking Union.

He is married to Lady Olivia Waldron, a past trustee of the Hunger Project Trust.

Extract from Debretts People of Today
1995 Ed. p1259

WALDRON, Victor Echevarri; s of Ernest Echevarri, ggs of Don Juan Ignacio Echevarri, of Bilbao, a Basque grandee and prominent activist in the Carlist uprising, who acquired British nationality in 1821 *Educ*. State Primary School (first wage earned at 14). WEA evening courses, West Ham College Summer School, King's College London University seminars... King Alfred Naval College, Officers' Training etc. B.A. failed, Harvard rejected, Queen's Birthday Honours under consideration... *"Never let your schooling get in the way of your education" Mark Twain*. M 1, 1947, Gladys Leila (d1953), o da of Col Sir William Waldron; 1 s (William b 1948), 1 da (Carola b 1953); m 2, 1955, Lady Olivia Elsie June, o da of 5 Marquess of Headfort (d 1960); 2 da (Sarah b 1956, Gina b 1957); *Career* serv RN 1940-45, Lt RNVR; memb Cons Central Office 1946-53, Parly candidate 1951, fin advsr to constituencies 1954; chm: Waldron Group of Cos, Roundwood Development Ltd; fndr dir Waldron Charity (private fndn); formerly: exec memb Nat Fedn of Property Owners, hon treas Property Cncl, dir The Hunger Project Tst; UK correspondent the Hunger Project Newspaper, ed Aware Digest 1988; author, journalist, news analyst and campaigner to end world hunger 1958-; Lionel Fifield Int Writers' award 1983; pres World Runners UK; pres Peterborough Benevolent Soc 1991-; memb: Dip and Cwlth Writers' Assoc, Foreign Press Assoc. Overseas Press Club of NY, Journalists Devpt Gp of World Aware, AAA, Sports Aid Fndn: Liveryman and Freeman City of London: FRGS; *Clubs* Naval and Military, United and Cecil, Royal Corinthian Yacht.

THE HUNGER PROJECT
AN ACKNOWLEDGEMENT TO JOAN HOLMES

She has inspired many, like myself, to become part of the great 'conspiracy,' i.e., to con-spire, to breathe together. We are together. We are the seed. The silent promise. We are the conspiracy of those who breathe together and who stand committed to have world hunger end, not just to be handled more effectively, but to be ended, finally, once and for all, forever.

To whom it may concern:

All of us are shaped, at least in part, by the thinking and writing of others. I have acknowledged many sources; others have become so much a part of me that where they end and I begin is lost. A little of each of them has become the whole of me. At the end of the day, to have repotted 'others men's flowers' has been a privilege that leaves me the richer, and I trust in no way diminishes them.

V.E.W.

The Beginning

On a spring day in 1980, forty people committed to the idea of ending world hunger in two decades, stood with me on Hampstead Heath. Three and a half hours later they had enrolled, at a face to face level, 679 people in the idea that the time had come to do exactly that.

One could fairly assume that if one in four people approached accepted this commitment, it would be true to say that in that period of time, approximately three thousand people on Hampstead Heath confronted world hunger at some level on that day.

To have made a similar impact with a traditional method would have necessitated hiring the Royal Albert Hall, finding a speaker good enough to fill it, plus all the costs of advertising, ticketing, servicing, etc., with a considerable doubt that at the end of the meeting an audience would have stayed around long enough to commit itself in such numbers.

It was my first experience of the power of the individual at work, and it became clear to me that, once we fully understand that we can make a difference, nothing can stand in our way.

"The simple awareness of this truth can produce a profound shift in the ability to get the job done."

"Where people lead and caring public opinion is strong, governments must pay attention," wrote Dame Judith Hart. Change comes from the initiative of people, not governments. Individuals making a difference have been responsible for every major change in the last twenty five years, and every movement – environmental, global, civil rights, women's rights, conservationists – has been people led. That is why individual enrolment involving face to face interaction had been the heart and soul of the Hunger Project since the days of its inception.

The Hunger Project is the 'enabling mechanism' which broadens the base and widens the understanding from which many organisations get increasing support, both in time and money.

Its business is to create a climate of opinion that requires acceptance of the idea that you are <u>responsible</u> for making the end of starvation an idea whose time has come.

Many who have never taken responsibility of any sort suddenly accept this, some without thinking, some without caring very much. For others it may be weeks, it may even be years before any need to honour this decision begins to germinate, but for all it is at this point that there is a strange alchemy in signing an enrolment card which in some way begins to work. At least that has been the experience of many people.

Without such commitment, our great grandchildren will still be sending food parcels to the starving in a world which will have decided that twenty million dying every year is a problem that it can live with. That for the first time in history of mankind (outside of war), not just poverty, but misery and degradation become acceptable rather than abnormal.

Robert McNamara, head of the World Bank, addressed three hundred International Bankers and concluded with the quotation:

"You see things as they are, and say 'Why?' I dream things that never were, and say 'Why not?' (McNamara quoting J.F. Kennedy during his Inaugural Speech, January 1960).

It is this vision that is empowering enough to involve you and in so doing involve you in your own fulfilment.

It gives you the commitment to challenge the accepted myths with which many people have been comfortable for so long. It invites you to invite them to join those who are committed to creating a world that will work.

There is massive evidence from many sources that testifies that a vision of a world free from starvation by the year 2000 is not an illusion, but a truth which time will confirm.

The first recorded question that was ever put to mankind, the question which has been hedged, dodged, avoided.

"Am I my brother's keeper?"

It remains for us to answer with a resounding YES!

Whatever you can do or dream you can, begin it.
Boldness has genius, power and magic in it. Begin it now.

Goethe

Mind and Heart – The Quest for Understanding

Despite the call of global economists for social justice and for bringing the poor under the protective umbrella of a fairer system, the political will necessary to achieve this continues to be resisted at the highest levels. The same lack of political will perpetuates the problem of world hunger, which in turn implies that those with power and influence are not prepared to come to the aid of the world's starving.

Attending a high-powered convention (as representatives of The Hunger Project) was to find speaker after speaker – African, American, European, Nobel Laureate, Economist or Parliamentarian – all unanimous in support of the statement that world hunger can be ended, and that political will is the missing factor in the ending of it.

On its way to becoming an overworked cliché, this lamenting of the lack of political will, seemingly ignores that will is the prerogative of the individual. It is the fight that the individual brings to this issue and cannot be legislated for and cannot be created by governments.

In a democracy, political will is engendered out of popular will and when expressed as public sentiment, it is the ingredient to which governments respond. The will of the people is the source of every Parliamentarian's power.

During this Rome Convention, learned speakers from various disciplines said much more on the theme – that the 'heart' is not enough, and what is required is cool, efficient analysis. For many people the first appeal is to the heart, and the need for understanding follows. Many are benumbed into indifference by the enormity of the facts that they have never been given an opportunity to comprehend.

Nevertheless, it is the 'heartfelt' concern about the problem of world poverty that becomes for many the beginning of commitment. Only when the old myths and assumptions are challenged is a new willingness created. The results when they come will be proof, if proof is needed, that where politicians may fear to tread, ordinary people do not and while they move governments it will only be as fast as they themselves move.

What is wanted and needed is information that puts the issue within the grasp of the man in the street, that calls forth a personal response out of which action is generated; not only more plans for the world's economy, but more commitment of the idea that hunger and starvation can be ended once and for all.

In Rome, Nobel Prize-winner Professor Leontief called for a cool economic analysis – only a difference of degree from the call made by Monsignor Nervo of Caritas, for education that brought the facts to ordinary people. This is the other side of the coin and not a different currency.

The handful of Quakers, who toiled for forty years to work into the consciousness of their nation the case against slavery, were unmoved by the powerful economic arguments produced by those cities whose continued prosperity depended on slavery. These arguments could not stand against the mandate of ordinary men and women, whose simple proposition was:

"This we will not have."

Hunger, like war, is too important an issue to leave to experts. The expert has to avoid the danger of being sucked into the belief that this problem can only be dealt with from the top down, and that those who contribute to the problem from the bottom up are of less relevance.

> There is a wide range of human concern, which involves commitment rather than detachment. What we, as persons, know of joy and compassion is as significant as anything we learn in the laboratory.

'Science and Religion' *The Times* 18.2.84

The improvement of the human condition is achieved when the heart, with its instinct for compassion, merges with the mind with its ability for economic analysis. The heart acknowledges that people do not die in millions – they die individually, personally, alone, each in his own particular way. The mind produces the problem solving know-how which is indispensable to saving these millions.

Together they can achieve what neither can do alone: transform the ending of world hunger into an idea whose time has come. Then we will know what we have done so far will not be lost.

Food Is The First Freedom

"Everything ripens at its time, and becomes fruit at its hour."

Victor Hugo's prophetic words on the power of an idea when its time has come have gone around the world, attached to various causes, but never to better purpose than in the case of ending hunger.

If ending world hunger has been the vision, then expressing it in Hugo's words as "an idea whose time has come" has been the banner that has rallied six million people in 130 countries.

One person in 1977 first shared their commitment to the end of hunger and starvation with another individual who shared, one by one, by one, individuals each expressing a personal commitment. Today individuals living in 138 countries have taken a stand by involving themselves in the Hunger Project.

In the Talmud, the earliest of Hebrew holy writ, appear the works "hakel lefee hazman" – "everything happens in its time." "To ripen in its time and become fruit in its hour," writes Tennyson, and with Victor Hugo, all proclaim that there is in the affairs of men an inexplicable natural progression of events which is not to be denied, there is a moment in or out of time when an idea's time has come, a moment when history plays its own hidden hand.

From biblical times to the middle of the last century, men found nothing abnormal about slavery, and had no difficulty in living with it. Then a sudden stroke of time and slavery became the great issue of their day. It took forty years to work into the consciousness of nations that the time had come for slavery to end. From where and why such an unstoppable resolve comes, cannot be explained. However powerful the criticisms and economic arguments, it was the mandate of ordinary men and women that prevailed.

Every generation makes its contribution to ongoing history, and the ending of hunger by the end of the century is the issue for us on this planet now. To that end, The Hunger Project has its own special role to play. Any suggestion that there is something bizarre or intimidating in being the focus for everyone who believes that death by starvation is a condition which does not have to continue, does not bear scrutiny. To anyone willing to admit that there have been sudden jumps in human history, such as the invention of agriculture, or the Industrial

15

Revolution, we now suggest a jump, far more concentrated and more intense, and of greater evolutionary importance.

We are entering a new period of history. All of mankind shares a single planet. We must find a way to make it work for all its people, if not, we are heading for the kind of disaster inconceivable before the splitting of the atom, (a fact that should concentrate our thinking).

The background in which The Hunger Project operates and on which its critics should judge it, is based on three basic tenets:

1. Because with all the countless, dedicated organisations and individuals working over the years, and with remarkable results, their work has produced what has been done to date, but it has not ended the persistence of hunger. In study after study, distinguished international commissions have come to one conclusion: humanity now possesses the know-how to end hunger, the key ingredient missing is the will to act on the ability, to put an end to starvation and hunger.

2. The Direct Aid Agencies throughout the world, with all the love, charity, and compassion at their command cover only 10% of the need, 'the tip of the iceberg'. To bring succour to 10%, to sixty million people, is a miraculous heart-warming achievement. For those who are starving now must be fed now: they cannot live on theories. However, the United Nations and World Bank statistics show another 520 million in dire need. These are malnourished millions whose quiet despair never makes a headline. These the Aid Agencies cannot reach, and their needs can only be answered by Governments and International Agencies. These are the voiceless and The Hunger Project is among the voices that speak for them.

3. Here at home, a recent survey shows that over 90% of devoted effort, time and money given to Direct Aid Charities comes from the 'church oriented'. This confirms our experience that there is a vast constituency of uncommitted men and women who have never been invited to be involved, and who are 'satiated into apathy' by the magnitude of a problem that they have never been given an opportunity to comprehend.

There is a new spirit gathering momentum. Now, whether you live in New York, Newcastle, New Delhi or New Zealand, you could be approached by a Hunger Project volunteer, invited to enrol, to take the 'End Hunger Briefing', and to understand that this is an issue in which you can make the difference. Wherever people gather, at railways, at bus stops, at festivals, you may find that this invitation comes from men and women volunteers whose own commitment leads them to tackle the first task which is <u>to broaden the base from which support is drawn, and to increase the awareness and the understanding of the need</u>. The second task is not to lament the lack of political will to end hunger, but to create that will, the popular and cumulative will. When this point is reached, our political leaders will find it worth their while to act.

Will cannot be generated by governments. Will is the gift that the individual brings to this and any issue. Every organisation that has advanced a cause in modern times, such as Conservation, Women's Lib, Ecology and Green Peace, CND, has been people led; created by individual will. None has been inaugurated by governments.

The willingness to interact face to face can only come from finding a volunteer force which has vision and commitment. Commitment for them is that which transforms a promise to reality. It is the daily triumph of integrity over scepticism.

In the idea that hunger can end men have glimpsed a vision of a world that can work. It is as if the threat of a nuclear dark age has moved men for new efforts. In a dark time, writes the poet, "the eye begins to see". To end world hunger by the year 2000 is achievable. It is not idealistic nonsense or Pollyanna sentiment.

For most men, the 'will to do good' runs deep and the need to help in time of famine is a strong moral obligation to which we add another dimension in the ending of hunger expressed by Victor Hugo:

Bridging the distance between the new initiatives in Europe and the apathy of the British Isles, like a beacon as Hugo's words:

> More powerful than a thousand
> armies is an idea whose time has come.

That hunger should end is an idea whose time has come, and millions are determined that starvation will not just be dealt with better, but ended once and for all. This is essential if our world is ever to be a morally habitable place.

Most men and women would prefer this problem to go away. A fiver to the vicar, a coin on flag day; they hope that will do the trick; but this is not to be and, if you are at this point of awareness, you may have reached the point of no return – that moment of which George Leonard speaks – a moment in or out of time when the context changes, when what seemed impossible becomes possible, and you find that you take responsibility for the world not only as it is, but as it could be.

Somewhere in all this is a cause big enough to turn your life around. Not a cause about charity or do-gooding, but about entitlement: the sharing of food, not by relief, but by entitlement, by justice, by right.

The House of Commons debates the problem of the human embryo and it fills the House politicians from all parties rush forth to demonstrate their concern on this issue of conscience. The claim that the embryo has certain inalienable rights seems unanswerable – the right to live, the right to be, the right to breathe. Surely, what must follow - as night follows day – is the right to eat, a fact which you and I take for granted from the moment of our birth. Our legislators <u>must</u> see this of equal concern!

"We live in a world without vision," wrote Barbara Ward. Without any sense of our mutual interest, and perhaps worst of all, without any moral conviction to sustain our Governments or direct our purpose. This is possibly the most dangerous situation in which human beings can find themselves. She went on, "Everything which works today began with a vision – a group of idealists prepared to work for it. We learn from visionaries; we don't learn from practical men of affairs. They are good once the direction has been set. You do not find them in the forefront."

We have reached the point of a change, a visionary change, and it starts as a gleam in one man's eye. We should remember that:

"The visionary is the true realist. Where there is no vision, the people perish."

Hunger for us in the West is a crisis of the spirit that needs more from us than our focus at a mental level. It is when you realise this that you take your stand and discover a new adventure in living, for to involve yourself in this issue is to involve yourself in your own fulfilment. It adds a transforming quality to your own life. A world in which hunger is ended is not merely different, it is a world transformed.

We have a world where six hundred million people awake each day to hunger. Increasing numbers of men and women have a vision of a world in which this does not have to be. But a vision without funding remains a dream, a pipe dream. The Hunger Project is not about dreams; it is about achieving the achievable.

"Hungry for money", is a criticism made against the Hunger Project by those who have forgotten how to ask for it. They shy away, intimidated from reminding any man that in the act of giving he achieves his own fulfilment. Perhaps they never quite dared believe it themselves. The church in particular has forgotten that it has a spiritual duty to put to a man that a preoccupation with 'making a living' should not be at the expense of 'making a life'. That working for money should not obscure the fact that your money should work for you. If your money works for you, you will have to accomplish that which brings joy into your life and in Group Captain Cheshire's words:

"It is in the solving of the problems of others that you find the answer to your own."

Many find the problem of world hunger so vast that they find escape in retreating into a position of indifference.

> The greatest enemy is inertia, and the sense that these problems are so complete that nothing we do can have any effect – the problems are far more profound and grave in their consequences for the future of this planet than the East/West divide.

> Dr Robert Runcie, Archbishop of Canterbury. 1981.

The Hunger Project speaks of a third way of giving. Not a gesture or a sacrifice, but a middle way, to give what is appropriate for you as an expression of yourself.

To be aware of the deeply satisfying privilege of giving at a level in which you experience your own 'wholeness'. It can be an act in which you yourself grow.

Only in a child is there an intact sixth sense of the one-ness of the world. For the young mind is not covered with onion-like skins of consideration and reasons and stuff which man must first peel away if he is to discover his real self.

A child has not time to ask if this deserving cause is more worthy than another deserving cause. He sees only the need and his response to it.

While man flounders around, relying on his brain box which is often overworked, overheated and often the centre of his apathy, the child has by instinct discovered more than charity and compassion – he has discovered communion.

We need to be willing to follow, to let our intuition guide us and to be willing to follow that guidance directly and fearlessly.

Shakti Gawain

It's Up To You

Last year, BBC's "Man Alive" produced a documentary called 'The Politics of Compassion.' The commentator in his final analysis on world hunger spoke of an opinion poll taken on the question, "Would you be prepared to pay some extra taxation if it went to end world hunger?" Alas, he said, only 33% of our uncaring nation said "Yes". Of a working population of approximately 23 million, in a time of recession and hardship, nearly one-third of our fellow countrymen would, according to that poll, elect to carry an extra tax burden for this end.

This generous concern is an expression of the power of the individual at work, and expresses his refusal to acquiesce in established injustices.

Many governments have been elected with less than a 33% vote in recent years. It is a challenge to all of them who fail in the humanitarian object of giving 1% of the Gross National Product to Third World Aid.

Where people lead and caring public opinion is strong, governments must pay attention. Once people understand that they can make a difference, nothing can stand in their way:

"the simple awareness of this truth can produce a profound shift in our ability to get every job done."

This change in the climate of opinion requires acceptance of the idea that you are responsible for making the end of starvation an idea whose time has come. When this is accepted, it becomes the conscious choice of people who are at the point of commitment, the point of no return, for commitment is the prerequisite and what then evolves is that you see what you can do and why and how you can effectively do it.

As we move from hesitancy to commitment, the context shifts and as we take responsibility for the world as it could be, so the doubts evaporate as to whether saying of world hunger:

"This we will not have" is enough, or if indeed anything, or that it can possibly contribute in any way to ending world hunger. That this is an idea whose time has come is simplistic, but any idea worth its salt must start from a simple premise. That an idea has truth, beauty and moral relevance is not enough for it to be taken up unless <u>its time has come</u> – only then does it become all powerful.

Who can doubt that men and women moved in this spirit, are in the spirit in which it will be done? The Bible, the Koran, the Torah, Upinashads, Sutras, etc., proclaim that men so moved will move mountains and this truth, seemingly so impractical and illogical, is manifest throughout history. It is part of man's enlightenment and is not now to be denied.

There is an ever-growing community drawn from many organisations, bodies and disciplines, who find their journey is over a common road and it is evident that in the last decade a powerful network of individuals has emerged. At a meeting, during a train journey, a party conversation, an expression is used, a glance exchanged, and recognition passes.

The people involved are in the areas of business, government, media, science, technology, education. They are people virtually aware of the critical issues of our time and are committed to resolve them. They represent a new and courageous initiative. In an endeavour to enhance the quality of life, they are the conspiracy.

They know that governments and international agencies can meet human need on the massive scale needed, but they will only act as fast as the people they represent move them.

The solutions will come out of the commitment of ordinary people who create the popular will and accept the challenge of making it good politics for our leaders to want to do something about it.

The ending of hunger is too important an issue to leave with governments and experts. There is room and work for all. Nothing is diminished in the sharing of it and the urgency demands that the question now be put that, if not now, When? If not here, Where? And if not you, Who?

From Gibran's *The Prophet* comes this thought:

All you have must one day be given.
Give now, so the season of giving may be yours
and not your 'inheritors'.

Ageing For Beginners

That the bittersweet rhythm of life itself can be disturbed by something so mundane as a communication from Her Majesty's Stationery Office is surprising. But there is one letter that comes to most of us demanding that we project ourselves into the future and make decisions in the now.

A few weeks before your 65th birthday, you are advised by HMG that you are about to reach the ranks of the elderly, implying that your active life is now over and your alternative choice is to accept a pension now, plus a free ride on the buses, or put it off another five years.

To say that this doom-laden correspondence is unwelcome to many is to say the least. You meditate on the passing of life and experience, the cold horror at the speed it went by. You wonder what happened to childhood, to youth, where all seemed possible, to the high ambition, and to the world waiting to be won. You reluctantly accept that on most issues the growing up process was in fact really giving up, and the feeling of being cheated arises from the secret conviction that only three weeks ago you were twenty-nine, or so it seemed. The years have gone and one knows not where.

In some future time the 'enlightened' government bureaucrat will perhaps write in a difference vein:

Dear Sir:

This is to remind you that you have now reached the age at which Churchill was first invited to become Prime Minister.

For you, not old age, but the golden age of man has been reached. Unlike anything that went before, you now have time to question and to seek justification of your very existence. Before that you were beset with problems, now you are free to give serious attention to yourself. With time on your hands you can seize the God-given opportunity of devoting it to enjoying the discovery of who it is, who has all this time.

This part of life is not like the others. You no longer need to do more and more of the same. Now your growing family is behind you and relaxation of your responsibilities lies ahead.

This is for you the Age of the Sage and the Seer. Now wisdom replaces knowledge and your Concorde pass, enclosed herewith, will send you back-packing to Kathmandu or California, where all good company men seek their spiritual leader, accept a discipline, ask all the questions and know who the questioner really is.

Yours faithfully,

A Civil Servant

That flight of fancy over, the train of thought persists.

"Can this part of your life really be used to make a difference in the world?" To paraphrase the poet:

"You pass this way but once," and to make some difference has a new urgency –

"For you pass not this way again."

Money is a hard taskmaster, dictating what you can or cannot do; always teasing you, tantalising you with dreams and wishes of the 'if only' that must remain a dream because you are preoccupied with making a living. You see things that are wrong and wish you had the power to change them.

The awareness grows that these limitations are no longer valid. Perhaps your money could work for you and accomplish what you want to accomplish. You recall reading words that stressed if money works for you, you will have enough, enough to accomplish that which brings joy into your life. Perhaps more, perhaps less, but if you have more prosperity with less, the net effect is more!

This man of the 'golden age' reflects on his new understanding that he is not so much in the world but of it, not something alien or other than the environment in which he lives, and that there is a mysterious inner core combining him to the rest of nature, the knowledge of which is powerfully contagious. To know that he is the tree in leaf, the grass that grows, the bird that sings, and the song it is singing, gives him dignity.

Now he must reject the call of the retiree's TV chair, waiting to feed pap to the mind that supposedly has no challenge, no goals, no interest. He rejects stamp collecting, bingo or painting by numbers, and looks afresh at what has to be done and how to do it.

So, late starter you may be, but not for you to sit around waiting for "The Great Reaper with as much equanimity as you can muster." Now your search for God is on. To help your fellow man is not a bad place to start.

You look at the great issues of your time. You have lived in a world where six hundred million awake each day to hunger and you experience gratitude for eighty years of life in which you have never known hunger, even for a day.

You sense that your shrinking world must be planned on the basis that we will all survive or none of us will. Hunger and starvation do not exist because the money supply is limited but because the abundance of money finances a world in which 20% of us consume 80% of the world's resources.

The problem is not academic. It is as pressing as the War/Peace issue, where the balance of terror holds the present pass. Hunger has an immediate urgency. Willy Brandt writes:

> Peace can never prevail while hunger rules. He that would ban war must first ban hunger. Morally it matters little if a human being dies in war or is condemned to starve to death because of the indifference of others.

From this grows a new-found social awareness and with it a man sees what needs to be done, and the need to do it.

There is no Jade Emperor in the sky,
There is no Dragon King on Earth,
I am the Jade Emperor, I am the Dragon King
So hold you hills and mountains I am coming!

Chinese peasant song

Ideas Have Legs

To stand up and be counted, to bear witness to a belief that world hunger can be ended by the end of this century, first appears to be the very antithesis of a genteel upbringing that taught you to keep your good works hidden.

The reason for change is that there is an urgent need to proclaim loudly, clearly, publicly, your belief that the will to have done with death by starvation is the missing factor in the ending of it. This will now proclaimed by you and others is a different ball game from whatever went before.

The World Bank calls for 1% of the GNP from the industrial nations of the world, a minimum necessary for the task of ending world hunger. Our leaders find this contribution too massive to contemplate. One-third of 1% now and an undertaking (not a commitment) to strive to reach 1% by the year 2000 is the best that can be done. A child giving one penny of the pound from its pocket money sees it for what it is – a trifling sacrifice towards achieving such great purposes.

Charity giving, even as a social gesture, is better than throwing up one's hands in despair. The problem is not so vast that all that can be done is to turn away. By retreating into a position of indifference, we become unconscious by choice. Does this reflect on our own aliveness? Is this the price we pay for it?

Many charities were staggered when a TV children's program launched a $100,000 appeal for the starving of Cambodia and this target was reached and passed, to the amazement of the adult world, by a further $2,900,000. The child has intact his sense of his world as the spaceship Earth. Hardly anyone seems to realise, writes Alan Watts:

> That this earth has always been in the sky, space is just as real as anything solid. Earth is in heaven. It spins, falls, floats in a spiral nebula. Earth is not opposed to heaven, it belongs in it as a member of the whole company of stars. We live on the side of our planet and look not up but out.

The child's mind cannot know all this intellectually. It just seems that they live as if they do.

"To go from unawareness to awareness produces a remarkable shift in the freedom people experience in being able to be who they are, in being able to live out their lives out of the knowledge that they make a difference and that is what their lives are about."

To discover commitment is to know the truth expressed by Goethe when he proclaims:

> Whatever you can do or dream you can, begin it.
> Boldness has genius, power and magic in it. Begin it
> now.

This 'now' means now! Now – now to be completely alive in the present, to live for the Now, and to understand that this is all there is. THIS IS IT, and there isn't anything else. The past is only 'today's remembrances', and the future but 'today's dreams'.

To understand that today is not a rehearsal for life; this is the main event; and to live as if you know that. To live now is to know that you are at any time but one heartbeat away from the finishing line in this particular race, and it adds an intensity and a transforming quality to life.

If you think that if Now is all there is to life, then this is a depressing thought. Perhaps you wish for something else, for something better. Perhaps you've clung to the hope of winning the pools or some other unlikely lottery because that's when you told yourself you would really start living! That's when you will really show 'em! All this is so much Fool's Gold.

Nothing is going to get better than this moment. To be here now – at this point in time's history – to be living, loving, longing, being, eating, seeing, knowing, laughing, wondering at this sheer breathtaking moment, this mysterious, exciting, contagious moment, when you, 'just little ol'e you', has been exalted enough to be part of the action, this must be enough for any of us.

The nature of a breakthrough is for you to stand on what you've gotten, what you've loved, what's been important to you, what's touched you, what's inspired you, what's turned your life on; to stand on that value you've already created for yourself and look out at the possibility for being alive that opens up, like a freedom, in front of you.

Werner Erhard

The Man With Cloth Ears

I first heard Joan Holmes speak of a third way of giving, not one of gesture or sacrifice, but a middle way – to give what is appropriate for you as an expression of yourself, to be aware of the deeply satisfying privilege of giving at a level in which you experience your own 'wholeness'. It can be an act in which you yourself grow.

I first heard her say this in the great hall of St Bartholomew's Hospital, which stands as it has since medieval times, close to St Paul's Cathedral in the City of London, where it has witnessed the Great Fire, the Plague and, in more recent times, the German firebombs. Its interior, with its high vaulted ceilings, is dominated by Holbein's famous portrait of Henry VIII, and before Joan Holmes spoke, my attention had wandered and I was completely taken up with these impressive surroundings.

I visualised that perhaps for us all there stood some great hall, some Valhalla in the sky, where we would soon check in, for the span of man's life is short. I looked again at the walls covered with rows of individual strips of age-darkened oak, each strip giving the name of some city worthy, Alderman, or Merchant Venturer, and the amount that he had given to creating this place – £50, £100, the occasional £1,000 ds – representing his generosity of his own day. I realised that it was possible that all other records of the lives of these men had now been lost in time. Only his name on the wall with the amount given remained for posterity to witness.

Would we too arrive at our own Great Hall to find Peter on the door, and hand in our own computer print-out, and to our chagrin realise that it contained no more than our name and an amount? Then question why this should be so? Why no other record of our achievements? What we had acquired, what we had built, what we had got, what we had achieved? Had the universal computer failed? Why no record of this? If not, not what you made, but what you gave, was the real measuring rod, and then some clearer direction along these lines should have been available. If, in fact, that was all there was to be programmed, it might have been made much clearer to men and women while they were on earth:

Patiently, Peter would listen, and reply:

"You should have known. Did we not send you prophet after prophet with this message?

"Indeed, at one time, for over thirty years we sent you the Son of Man himself. How can you say you were not told? Did you develop cloth ears down there?"

"Now," he said, "you go over there, get into the right queue because you are going round again. I have endorsed your print-out to ensure that you will again have two ears and one mouth, and next time please try listening twice as much as you speak!"

The imaginative soliloquy over, I came back into the room to hear Joan say:

"Prosperity should be a joyous experience for a free person."

To want bread for myself is a
material need. To want it for my
brother is a spiritual one.

Dostoevsky

Loyalty to a petrified opinion
never broke a chain
or freed a human soul.

Mark Twain

The Grandfather's Tale
(with apologies to Geoffrey Chaucer)

To my grandchildren:

It will be some years before this letter is very meaningful for you and before you have any understanding of these moments when our minds stretch out and touch across the line of time.

Let me tell you something of our world as it is to me, and of the moment when suddenly and mysteriously the context in which I saw it shifted, and I found myself taking responsibility for this planet, not only for what it is, but for what it could be.

To see ourselves as others see us is an early lesson in life and my story starts with a recent visit we had from a little E.T. – a delightful extra-terrestrial little chap who came, to the delight of millions who watched it at the cinema. He stayed but a short time, and with the help of his earthling friends, beat a hasty retreat.

His departure was not altogether surprising, for through his eyes he saw our spaceship, 'Earth', as if it were a village of one hundred people and he saw that six possessed half the wealth, and ninety-four existed on the other half. The richest twenty-five would live into their seventies in comfortable old age and the poorest fifty-five would die before fifty and two of their children would die before reaching the age of five. Seventy would live and die without ever knowing that they too were on a spaceship and a quarter of the whole village would suffer malnutrition year in and year out.

So, it is no wonder that he found it intolerable to stay as one of the affluent few, or one of the impoverished many, and he decided to take the first opportunity to leave us. We are, of course, not a village of a hundred people. We are 4.6 billion, but nearly a billion of us live in abject poverty, so the rest of his equation was quite true.

As he disappeared into space, many of us were left wondering what life is like on a spaceship, for we had forgotten that it is exactly like now, that our own earth has always been in the sky, so superbly designed that for over two million years humans have been here without ever knowing they were aboard ship. The space we move in as real as anything solid. Earth is in heaven. It spins, falls, floats, in a spiral nebula. Earth is not opposed to heaven; it belongs to it as a member of the whole company of stars.

"We live on the side of our planet and we look not up but out," writes Alan Watts.

Right now we are travelling at 60,000 miles an hour in a great vastness of space. The sun flies in company with us, just at the right distance to keep us alive. We are a tiny speck, only 8,000 miles in diameter, and so extraordinarily well invented that until recently, world man has been flying on automatic pilot. Now that time has been long enough and you and I are part of the new-age and ready to take control and be responsible for the future of our seen and unseen universe.

You too will have your problems; that is why we are all here. Men and women are problem-solvers. This is the whole reason for these precious seventy years – give or take a few – in which we work out our destiny. Our very *raison d'être* for the whole of this time is for us to solve the problems of our age.

What yours will be exactly, I do not know. But my grandfather lived until the end of the last century, and he lived to see the end of slavery. The ending of it for him was an idea whose time had come.

As your grandfather, my contribution to ongoing history I hoped was to see hunger and starvation end, and to know that you will come of age in a world without hunger. There will be other injustices – other inequities, other wrongs – to which you will give your attention in your own good time, and more than any other generation before you, you will be armed with such new technology, such problem-solving science, the like of which it is not even given for me to guess. What will always bind us across space is that you will be fortified by the old truths. These are continuously powerful and they pass like golden thread through one generation to another. What was just a vision for me is expressed in Gibran's *The Prophet*. "That it is enough for those who have deserved to drink from the ocean of life to fill their cup from your little stream." This I hope will become a code for you to live by.

It will be for you to discover something that I only suspect, that what it means to be human and what it means to be divine are one and the same. Man has a divine destiny as a problem solver, confirmed in HOLY WRIT. Jesus said, "In as much as you do it unto one of the least of these, my brethren, you do it unto Me."

From Where I Sit:
Agony And Ecstasy Of Fund Raising

So you would like to lead a contribution meeting?

"Yes," he said, eyes ashine with commitment, "but I need to know the case I argue and to be sure that what I say does justice to the stand I have taken!" "If," he asked, "you were in my audience, what would you want to hear me say?" Firstly, remember, from the moment of inception, the Hunger Project has been true to its vision, that vision held by us all to be a self-evident truth that hunger should end, not just be dealt with better, not just handled more effectively, but ended finally once and for all, and forever. This has been the vision to which we are committed.

Joan Holmes recently met with members of the World Bank and they raised the question as to whether the ending of hunger by the year 2000 was American optimism. In their view it could be 2005 or 2010.

It would not have been political in the middle of such a serious discussion to have reminded them that five years ago, any suggestion that hunger could end received either a patronising pat on the head or strongly expressed disbelief that hunger, starvation, famine which have been with us from the beginning of recorded time should not be a permanent part of our world.

It would have been counter-productive to have reminded them of this, but that is no reason why we should not remind ourselves how far along this road we have travelled in the last five years.

Increasing numbers of people recognise that in a world that can put men on the moon it is an abomination that a child should die in the arms of an emaciated mother for the want of sustenance. This view has never existed so powerfully, for it is more alive today that it has ever been.

It is from this belief that you rise to face your first contribution meeting. This new experience you will find surprisingly moving. Here, for the first time, people have come not only to hear you; and there is not one of them who could not have been doing something other than listening to you, something with their family, or in their garden.

So many calls on their time! Yet they have not only come, but they have come to give their money. The quality of your audience and the quality of their commitment suddenly hits you.

You will then find it in you first to express your acknowledgement of those who over the years have given their lives to this issue. Historically, looking back at whatever efforts were made, and there were many, you can acknowledge the churches of all denominations who long before the advent of Oxfam, Christian Aid, Save the Children or the Hunger Project, have for generations – and often alone – through their missionaries taken the full brunt of the poverty and ignorance of the hungry world.

The Direct Aid agencies who are the successors of this work take on the day to day problems of the Third World and our world stands in their debt.

They are for the most part manned in the field by men and women of great compassion and understanding, and the administrators at home are men and women of great ability and deep commitment.

The Direct Aid agencies claim that on a global basis they bring succour to 10% of the hungry. This is the great silent majority of the malnourished whose quiet despair never makes the headline, the silent ones, whom the aid agencies cannot reach, who have no spokesman and for whom we in the Hunger Project are but one voice.

It is in your favour that what you have to say has more than truth and moral relevance, these alone are not enough. You also have an idea whose time has come, and because it has this extra factor, it is achievable. Everything happens when its time has come. Make no mistake, in this matter you are on the side of the angels, a fact that is empowering beyond your dreams. What next emerges is the understanding that, in the West, hunger is a crisis of the spirit. It needs more than your mental focus if you are to be more than a purveyor of idle dreams. This is the point where your commitment is tried and the now familiar words of Hugo, that "an idea whose time has come is more powerful than a thousand armies", is ready to be battle tested, and you with it.

If you have never asked for money it is a considerable experience, bringing you many new insights into human nature. The fact is that by involving yourself in this asking process you are stretching your own horizons, you are an advocate of a world where hunger is ended and this is a world that is not only different, it is transformed. This involves you in your own fulfilment. The reason for your presence on the platform is in itself a statement that you know the problem of hunger is not only a problem for the hungry, it is also your problem. You not only know this but you live your life as if you know it.

Money, as most of us know, is a hard taskmaster. It dictates what you can or cannot do, always teasing you, always tantalising you with wishes of the 'if only...' that must remain a dream. You see wrongs that you would like to cure and you wish you had the power to change them.

Hunger does not exist because of a shortage of money. The money supply is unlimited, it is the abundance of money that finances a world in which 20% of us in the West consume 80% of the world's resources. No one starves in the world because of a shortage of money. On any given day, in any great city, millions of pounds change hands in staggering amounts. There is a great abundance of money, much of which is beyond the abilities of Chancellors, Exchequers or Parliaments to control.

You are going to ask a man to do more than give his money, you are asking him to change his relationship with it. As you do so, you present him with new issues requiring a new viewpoint. He has been asked before for money; now he is challenged to give, not as a gesture, and not as a sacrifice, but you invite him to a middle way, to give an amount that is worthy of him, an amount that can express his 'wholeness', something that adds to his own growth process. This is something startling and new.

Men do have strong views about money. You soon discover how articulate they are. Fear of being conned goes deep. There is no activity or satisfaction man would not forego before his money.

The questions will come thick and fast – what do you want money for? – put in such a way that you are on the defensive. The questions and the questioner are uncomfortable.

"Charity begins at home," is the viewpoint of many for whom charity also ends at home, and is only acceptable from those who are committed to home charities.

"Leave us alone," will come from your businessmen friends, "let us get on with our jobs, let us make our profits, eventually the benefits will trickle down to the poor and hungry." In the sixties and seventies many of us were committed to the 'trickle down' theory until it became obvious it did not work.

It is true that many rich men go to the grave without experiencing their own abundance or even their own sufficiency. Too often their riches have them rather than they have their riches. This is why so many of them are prepared to be generous at the expense of their heirs and why charities have such extensive legacy departments. The 17th century poet, Silesius, wrote:

> A wealthy man obsessed
> with profits, deals and losses
> is a poor wretch,
> possessing nothing,
> he is in truth a man possessed.

At the other end of the equation you have a trade unionist he would declare 1% of his income after tax to be a derisory increase, not worth having if negotiated by his trade union leader. If you suggest that he might now give it away, this is to see it leap from the insignificant to the massive in the mind of a potential giver.

Your audience can now be reminded that if they are going home to a refrigerator full of food, or at least half full, in the context of the world of which you have been talking, this is comparatively such abundance, you are really talking to a room full of millionaires. It is good for them to understand that is how you, in front of the room, see them and it is good for them to see themselves in such a role.

You will meet indifference. There are millions committed to the status quo and they are doing all right in the world as it is, and have little commitment to change. Apart from those who believe in the 'trickle down' theory, there are others who are convinced that our world is like a lifeboat loaded to the gunwales and, however much pity there may be around for those men, women, and children swimming around out there without hope, any suggestion that they should be pulled on board will only result in sinking us all, and this they see as a dangerous doctrine.

This you challenge, for the only boat available to us all is our 'Spaceship Earth'. If we are fortunate enough to be on the upper decks, then to waste time putting out the deck chairs and to leave the passengers travelling steerage with a hold filling with water and unworkable pumps, is to say the least, short-sighted. In fact, a disaster course of Titanic proportions.

Then you have those who are convinced that their indifference to this issue costs them nothing. Their mistake is to imagine that an issue of this magnitude, (which some would describe as the most important of our age) and of which they choose to be unconscious, not alive to, can only mean that some part of them is dead. This is an option they can choose but there is a price to be paid, and that price is paid in their own aliveness.

This 1% of the nation's Gross National Product is the figure needed by the World Bank from governments in the developed world if hunger is to be ended. Our government failed to meet this figure, they also find it too large a sum to be considered. One-third of 1 % is as close as we can get as a nation.

I know from my experience the constant battle I have had to change my relationship with my own money. I recall with embarrassment the difficulty and upset that arose between my wife and I when, during the Cambodian crisis, she sent to Oxfam a three figure cheque. This seemed to me thoroughly unreasonable. The Waldrons were always in the fiver-and-occasional-tenner class and this sort of behaviour seemed highly irresponsible. There was no argument so absurd that I did not pursue it, even to suggest that three figure cheques might be considered vulgar. All of this was a hangover from what I call the BWE years (before Werner Erhard, from whom I first learned something about money and my relationship with it).

Since the end of the tithe, (the legally enforced 10% to the established church), the church has forgotten how to ask for money. They shy away, intimidated from reminding a man that in the act of giving he achieves his own fulfilment, perhaps never quite believing it themselves.

Their willingness to accept with gratitude, metaphorically touching the forelock for whatever pittance has come their way... The widows mite is acceptable to the glory of God, the Duke's fiver is not. Some priest, somewhere, someday, will be ready to take back to his richer parishioners their cheques and to explain patiently that little gestures do no honour to the cause and, as such, demean the giver.

Giving as a gesture is a cop-out, it gives you no experience of your own abundance or even your own sufficiency. It does not express who you really are, and you do no justice to yourself. Perhaps a silent moment with the Duke to see if, given a chance, 'out of the still quiet voice', might come a different cheque, one that he finds on reflection, he could live with.

Finally, I would remind you how Joan Holmes summarised her own position:

"When I signed the enrolment card, I did not sign up to give my money to the end of hunger and starvation. I signed up originally to give my talents and my ability and my time. I thought I was giving so much of these things that I wouldn't also need to give my money.

When I recognised that I had the opportunity to channel my money in the direction of having the world work, it changed my life. I was the person who always had visions and dreams. I don't know who I thought was going to fund them but I knew it wasn't me. It didn't occur to me that when someone really cares about something they put their money behind it, when someone really wants to have an impact on something they put their money behind it.

I discovered I could write a cheque to the Hunger Project and take responsibility for financing my dream. In other words, I grew up enough to be able to put my money where my commitment was and it changed my life."

For me, an older generation, at the end of the day the truth is in the words of Gibran's *The Prophet*:

> All that you have shall one
> day be given. Therefore give
> now, that the season of giving
> be yours, and not your inheritors.

Now, if you are ready, the room is set up. The team supporting you are in their places. The backsides are all on the chairs, so go to it! Before rising to speak, pause for a moment. Have a sense of who you are and what your business is about. So it can be said of you, and of those to whom you are speaking, that by the end of the evening they truly understand, in Gibran's words, that:

> Those who have deserved to
> drink from the ocean of life
> have a right to fill their
> cup from your little stream.

Reflections On The New York Marathon

Man's power to reflect is a power that he has above any other species on this planet.

The evening before the New York Marathon – the nervous excitement before the big day, the hall filling with people, the buzz of conversation – momentarily my mind drifts back to my first visit to this great city.

As a young naval officer arriving from blacked-out Europe to this haven of light and plenty, it was as if I had stepped onto another planet. Behind this brightly lit facade was the serious business of transporting three million fighting men (the largest force ever to cross an ocean) to the battle zone. The new world coming to the succour and support of the old, and in so doing creating a deep, lasting bond between us.

The sudden realisation that I was involved in a war to end starvation in the world with the sons and daughters of the men who forty years earlier I had possibly conveyed across the seas, gave me a sense of continuity, companionship, "I have known you all before," feeling.

The knowledge that this struggle would also be won in no small part by the new technology, which had already made what had once seemed impossible become possible.

I recalled another time, another place, when technology changed the course of history. A grey North Atlantic, a darkened ship, cold mist, drifting fog and two thousand cramped, restless, stomach-queasy GI Joes below decks. Two days out of New York full ahead into the deep swell, the look-outs doubled, muffled with their binoculars peering into the Arctic night.

This was the first voyage on which we carried a newly installed piece of technology called R.D.F. (Radar Direction Finder), later to be known as RADAR, an ugly lighthouse-like construction built behind the bridge, and the watch-keeping officer was only just discovering the revolutionary effect it was to have on navigation.

A Bridge telephone rings:

"RDF reporting, Sir – strong echo – dead ahead – 10 miles – possible iceberg."

Stooping over the dimly lit chart table, the navigator immediately plots the position.

" How's her head, quartermaster?" and the crisp response comes at once from the man at the wheel.

"Steering 060, Sir."

"Change course to starboard, steer 065."

And the ship responds, comes into her new course, a change barely perceptible even to those on the bridge. Moments later, again the voice from the helmsmen:

"Now steering 065, Sir."

"Steady as she goes quartermaster."

"Steady she is, Sir," comes the response.

Four authoritative commands, and a new piece of technology became part of our lives. A situation which, thirty years earlier, had led to the Titanic disaster, now dealt with by a simple five degree change of course.

My daydream ended. The meeting started and the analogy became clear. Tomorrow most of the people in the room would have run through the streets of New York in front of a million people with the message, 'End World Hunger', a message which thirty years earlier would have expressed no more than a well-meaning sentiment, but today, backed with modern technology, was within our grasp.

In the past the sheer immensity of the problem made it 'ungraspable' and even now the suggestion that we could change opinions and create the popular and political will in the world seems unrealistic.

How are we going to change the thinking of millions, alter priorities of whole nations? The answer is clear. We are not! We could not! And indeed we do not need to do so. A five percent shift, a five degree change in the disaster course on which humanity has set itself, is all that is required.

We are part of that unique five percent. And we are not running as an expression of a pious hope. We are not the purveyors of idle dreams. We are the achievers of the achievable, and tomorrow we run in the knowledge that that's who we are.

Fifty Years On

The Sinking of the Windsor Castle by Enemy Action

North Africa March 23rd 1943

Prologue

History records that by the end of the second world war, the largest single body of fighting men, some three million, had been transported across the oceans of the world to various battle fronts. For the most part this was the New World coming to the support and succour of the Old, and to defend the civilisations in which they also had their own deep roots.

This is the final episode in the life of one ship engaged in this task and of its Captain.

By 1943 under the command of Captain J C Brown, RNR, RD, the Windsor Castle, a former mail ship on the Cape route, had long since been stripped of her luxury fittings and her distinctive Union Castle livery concealed under a drab coat of battleship grey. The ship had already seen active service as a front line transport, moving men from the UK to North Africa under its newly appointed American Commander in Chief, General Dwight D Eisenhower.

After the first landing in Algiers, and as the advance across Africa continued, the ship was detailed for special duties. Infantry reinforcements were urgently required to strengthen the front line, and to support the less experienced Allied troops whose advance had been halted following their first clash with the battle-tested panzers of General Rommel.

The urgent need for these reinforcements to secure the front line involved the use of fishing ports totally lacking any big ship facilities and where ships of the size of Windsor Castle had been unknown.

After steaming through the night in company with a destroyer escort, the big ship arrived off a tiny fishing port in adverse weather involving high winds and heavy seas. The approaches were littered with wrecks and other obstructions and a decision had to be made as to how, and at what point, the ship could reasonably make her hazardous entry into the mini-port.

On the bridge a state of tension existed as the Captain weighed the need to put the fighting men ashore as against the risk of damaging his great ship, which appeared to dwarf the small town. There ensued a delay with everyone hoping for a break in the weather. Then from the bridge came the Captain's voice calling for silence. With his Bible, which was never far from his side, now held closely, he prayed. After a minute or two he arose and without hesitation ordered "slow ahead both engines", set the course and passed safely through the many obstructions to berth safely at the jetty.

The human cargo was safely discharged and under cover of darkness the ship left harbour and ran at full speed through the night to Algiers, closely guarded by her destroyer escort.

As the newly appointed RNVR officer responsible for the ship's defence, I was presumptuous enough to later remark to the Captain that I thought taking the Windsor Castle in and out of that difficult situation without the aid of tugs, was a fine display of seamanship. I recall his impatient reply, "Guns, learn that there are moments when God is at the helm of this ship."

With the cynicism of youth I said to myself , "O' Captain, my Captain, how grateful I am that you were also present."

Night Attack

To the Fourth Sea Lord's Office at the Admiralty in London on a March evening came an action report to the effect that:

"On the morning of March 23rd Convoy steaming in three columns with his Majesty's transport Windsor Castle leading the starboard column 10 and 31 zigzag number 12 position 8 miles south west of position K, the convoy came under air attack which included low flying twin-engined torpedo-carrying aircraft. Their attack concentrated on the Windsor Castle and she was hit on the port side by aerial torpedo causing immediate flooding to the engine room and number four hold (time 02.30). A damage report indicated that the ship was in imminent danger of sinking. The Captain thereupon ordered 'abandon ship', which evolution was carried out in an orderly manner."

This type of report was only too common during those years. It was duly acknowledged, filed, and became just another wartime statistic.

Now let me relate what it meant through the eyes of the people involved.

The sudden shock of the explosion shattering the night, the strident notes of the alarm bells; the deck mustering of disciplined fighting men; and the strange silence as the convoy left the sinking ship behind and disappeared over the horizon.

Even with disciplined personnel the manning and launching of lifeboats under such conditions is never a simple operation. Where there were insufficient lifeboats, the ship was amply supplied with life rafts which only required to be launched over the side. The life-jacketed men leapt into the water and swam to them. Being blessed with fine weather this was not so difficult an undertaking as it sounds. There were quite a few experienced seamen (some had been torpedoed more than once) who preferred to take their chance on a life raft rather than scramble into an overloaded boat.

For a time after the attack the guns crews remained at their posts and on three occasions during the night alarms were sounded in anticipation of enemy aircraft. The Luftwaffe seemed satisfied with the night's work and made no further attacks on the convoy, and the destroyer escort returned to rescue survivors and defend the stricken ship if necessary.

To those of us still on board it seemed unbelievable with the ship now settling at such an angle and with the holds filling fast, that she would not plunge to the bottom at any moment.

John Watney, Naval correspondent of the Sunday Express thirty years ago, wrote of this incident and referred to the ship as being an extremely "lucky ship". An expression I do not think Captain Brown would have used, but he would not have quarrelled with his own statement that it seemed that Providence had taken some special interest in this ship. He had been heard to say a number of times that "God was at the helm" and that no harm could come to his ship while he was in command.

The toughest old "shell back" among the experienced members of the crew had come to believe that, if nothing else, their captain's religious commitment was in itself a useful extra insurance against the perils of war!

Watney wrote of other episodes when the ship, left Canada unescorted, she relied on her speed to avoid the U-boat across the shipping lanes. Again Captain Brown prayed. Then an out-of-season fog descended and enshrouded the ship, staying with her all the way across the Atlantic – a nice 'personal' fog on the otherwise clear ocean and thereby shielding the speeding ship from a U-boat's probing periscope.

There was also the story of the Captain's bomb. In harbour during an aerial bombing, a bomb had penetrated the dining saloon close to the Captain's table, It did not explode and under his calm instructions, (Captain Brown was at all times completely unflappable) the damage control team removed it, and pitched it overboard like so much galley garbage.

On board the Windsor Castle the remaining drama was rapidly being played out. Boats were launched and soon loaded to the gunwales, life rafts thrown overboard and men jumped into the sea to be hauled aboard anything that floated. Eventually the Chief Officer reported to the Master that everybody had got away and would he now leave with them? Standing with his Bible under his arm and with calm authority he declined, adding that the boat was to be taken away from the side to rescue as many people as possible, He added that he would stay to the end and if she went quickly would make for a life raft.

Orders were then received by the three destroyers to attempt to take the ship in two. Captain Brown who had remained on board with a handful of officers and men, seeing she was settling rapidly ordered the naval party to be taken off at once. The last naval rating slid down the rope from the bows on to the deck of the destroyer. Captain Brown then joined the last lifeboat, he accomplished this as calmly as everything else he did and on reaching the boat casually flipped some grit from his uniform jacket and commented "there she goes we left that a bit close didn't we".

As if waiting to be assured of the captain's safety and not wanting to delay the final act, the great ship hung at an almost perpendicular angle as if taking a last bow. Then her final agony came in the form of the strident hiss of escaping compressed air echoing across the water to the silent watchers in the boats.

Epilogue

This was not my last contact with a remarkable man, who, fifty years on has still left me with an indelible impression of his personality.

A few weeks later I was in London waiting to join another ship and on passing the YMCA Office in Piccadilly saw a large poster announcing a meeting that day "God's Hand Among the Convoys" – speaker Captain J C Brown, RNR.

Delighted and surprised at this opportunity to greet my last captain once again I entered the hall as the meeting began.

When Brown saw me he summoned me to the platform and said the reunion was no coincidence but another example of how God worked.

After the meeting, I put to him a question that had been puzzling me – How did he explain the sinking of a ship that had God's special protection?

Without hesitation he replied that this lesson in humility was one for him to learn. It was not a question of asking "too much of God"; only "a humble and contrite heart was needed", Perhaps we had lost sight of that! That episode was a test of faith and was, for him, a renewal and had in no way diminished his own faith.

My naval service was limited to the period of "hostilities only". I still wonder if there is something different about men who go down to the sea and ships and see the works of the Lord, even in wartime. Perhaps even more so in wartime.

J C Brown believed in what he saw as a basic truth. The mind of God was available for the mind of Men, and in moments of quiet, meditation, or prayer one could get closer to God than to oneself. This is not something to which he gave mere lip service. He not only believed this as a truth but lived out the whole of his life in this belief. To him, "when men listen God speaks", was a maxim for life.

You are not enclosed within your body,
nor confined to house, or fields, that which
is you, dwells above the mountain and roves
with the wind. It is not a thing that crawls
into the sun for warmth, or digs holes into
darkness for safety, but a thing free, a spirit
that envelopes the earth and moves in the ether.

The Jogger's Charter

An Interview With Tom Knight of *Running Magazine*

Hyde Park, regular jogger, Victor E. Waldron, businessman, property company director, freelance writer, Member of the Diplomatic and Commonwealth Writers and the Journalist Development Group of CWDE, and UK President of World Runners, an international running club with 12,000 members in thirteen countries, talks while jogging with Tom Knight.

TK: Your interest in running started with the impression that the 1936 Berlin Olympics made on you. That's a long time ago. What do you do now as a senior citizen?

VEW: Yes, it was a long gestation period. The catalyst came at the age of sixty-five, you get this letter from the Ministry of Health and Social Security implying that your active life is now over and asking if you would like to take your basic pension. This arrives when many feel they are at the very height of their powers. It should really remind every new pensioner that he has reached the age at which Churchill was first invited to be Prime Minister of Great Britain, and not 'old age' but a new 'golden age' is about to begin.

TK: What part does jogging play in your life and what influence does it have on your day to day decisions?

VEW: I am aware that for every hour I jog it is one week less in a geriatric ward. It is certainly easier and cheaper to keep well than it is to get well and I am grateful for the good health that I have enjoyed through life. Jogging does play a part in my philosophy for living. Life is in fact a four-lap race... the first lap through childhood and adolescence, the second through maturity, the third through middle age with its successes and failures, a growing family behind you and a relaxation of your business responsibilities. And the fourth and final lap is the one that makes sense of the other three, when you seek to understand what the race was all about. Not to know this moment would be to half live, to shrink away as something unhealthy or abnormal would rob this part of life of its purpose.

TK: That's an interesting idea, life as a four-lap race. Have you ever thought of writing a Jogger's Charter expressing such a philosophy?

VEW: For me it is not just the health, mental and physical satisfaction, I add an extra motivation to my running. You know, every World Runner's vest carries the message, 'End World Hunger'. Last year, passing cheques totalling £56,000 to Sport Aid was very satisfying. As UK President, I led a team of eighty-nine World Runners to Moscow, the largest single contingent from the West, to run with this same message which was written in Russian. To have a group of Russian athletes around a piano in a hotel and to teach them to sing "We are the world... " would have warmed Bob Geldof's heart. Last year World Runners was invited by the Tunisian Ministry of Sport to organise its first marathon which was a privilege, it has now become an annual part of the Tunisian sports scene.

TK: A running club which is not exclusively about running will always seem a bit strange to athletes, don't you think?

VEW: Every Sunday, under Tim Flach's training, we have a mixed squad of very serious runners who appear in AAA events and produce very good times. Running, like no other sport, has the power to move people. It is such a demonstration of commitment. The end of a marathon will find both runners and supporters in tears. It's a highly charged moment when men and women discover that their limitations are exactly that, their limitations, imposed on themselves by themselves. They have gone beyond what they thought were their limitations. Running a marathon is a discovery of oneself.

TK: Many runners are sponsored for many charitable good causes. Why do you think that the issue of world hunger should have a special place?

VEW: Since the beginning of history runners have always carried the good news, and the good news of our time is that hunger can be ended in our lifetime.

TK: Do you think running with a message does anything to end hunger, apart from the sponsorship money that you raise for the direct aid agencies?

VEW: Hunger persists for one reason and that is the lack of political will to have it handled. Political will is created out of the popular will. The 'end hunger' message must become part of the fabric of our society. When we run, we are not expressing some sentimental codswallop. This is the message of the Brandt Commission which it took seventeen leading statesmen two years to come up with. It's also the message of the Manifesto Against Hunger, now signed by 78 Nobel Laureates, which World Runners relayed across Europe and through America at the time of the Olympic Games. It is the opinion of the American Academy of Science and many other organisations.

TK: It is a bit visionary for some people. You think it is more than just expressing a pious hope?

VEW: For me. Edward Heath said in 1984:

"To organise a run to end world hunger conveys to me the sense of urgency which all decent people must feel about the problem". And Sir John Cumber, Director General of Save the Children, called World Runners, "the only club dedicated to ending hunger through running, it is a wonderful concept." And I particularly value Geoffrey Cannon, writing in *Running Magazine* in 1983, when he said, "To be a member is to be borne upon a tide of fellowship." For me, that was true then and it is true today.

No longer conscious of my movements I discovered a new unity with nature. I have found a new source of power and beauty, a source I never dreamed existed.

Roger Bannister
On breaking the four-minute mile

Run For Your Life!

The active man's first brush with old age comes as a shock and from a least expected quarter. Some weeks before his 65th birthday, on a morning like most others for men who are deeply immersed in doing what is on reflection just more and more of the same, the postman delivers to the Welfare State man, a communication from Her Majesty's Government. This is an advice that in a few weeks you reach the ranks of the O.A.P.s, and lists the dubious benefits that go with this privilege.

The first reaction is horrific. Disbelief followed by the realisation that, having reached the age at which Churchill was first summoned to become Prime Minister, you are offered a pittance and a free ride on the buses.

The reality of this official announcement, that active life is now ending and that this has happened almost without one perceiving that it has passed, is undeniable. Reflecting that it seemed to one's mind but three weeks ago that one was twenty-nine, and now the sudden realisation that the years have gone and one knows not where.

What happened to youth and the promised childhood where everything seemed possible and the whole world was there to be won? What happened to the high ambition, to those days of astounding adventure which began so promisingly eighty years ago? Was this all forgotten, condemned as naïve by the adult world? How much of growing up was in fact really giving up?

Strange it is that only in the West is age treated as an affliction, that here men are persuaded by the media that the little of life left in retirement is for pottering over the jobs one had told oneself for years one had not had the time to tackle, now was the opportunity to do so many of them, and yet the truth is that most times the garden shed will still go unpainted. The chair in front of the television will do overtime and the great one-eyed monster will feed pap to the mind that now has no challenge, no action, no goals, no decisions, no interest, and men await with *such equanimity as they can muster, the arrival of the Great Reaper*. Meanwhile, anything, any hobby, any collections, bingo, stamp collecting, painting by numbers, to crowd out the waiting spectre of death.

That the curve of life peaks around thirty is a truth and to dress in track suit and to jog through the country and to experience physical fitness is not to deny this. To find that the body can respond at the age of sixty-five to exercise that seemed beyond it at fifty-five and most certainly would not have been attempted at forty-five, is its own reward. This does not mean that one seeks merit in acting out a role outside ones age. It does mean that physical well-being brings with it a mental alertness, an aliveness that could initiate not old age but the golden age of man.

The understanding that life is a four lap race. The first lap through childhood and adolescence, the second lap through maturity, family and responsibilities, the third through middle-age with its successes and failures, a growing family behind one, and the slow relaxation of the responsibilities that were involved. Now the fourth, final leg of the race, the one that makes sense of all the other three, the lap of fulfilment, the understanding of what the rest were all about. The pace quickens to go for the tape, to know the finish will give point and understanding to the others and "not to know this moment would be to half live, and to shrink away is something unhealthy, abnormal and would rob this part of life of its purpose" – wrote the philosopher Douglas Harding.

Nevertheless, it is not necessary for this part of life to be just like the others. Now man has the time to question and to seek the justification for his existence.

"Before this he was beset with problems; now he is free to give serious attention to himself and with time on his hands can seize the God-given opportunity of devoting it to enjoying the discovery of who it is who has all this time. " – Douglas Harding.

Few men see this challenge, and if outwardly one appears of less use, now inwardly he is a free spirit that can arise to new heights.

The atoms, proteins, molecular energy cells, which make man give him a mysterious core binding him to all the rest of nature. To understand that we did not so much come into this world but out of it, that one is not something alien or imposed on this planet for a limited period, that man is as right as the galaxies in the heavens, the stars in the sky, the grass that grows, the birds that sing and the song they are singing. This awareness that his sun/energy field which was the start of all life on this planet, does not disappear into nothingness. That one is not in the world but *of* the world.

This is true of what men know of their origins and to be in accord with this knowledge is both mysterious and powerfully contagious. It is true of our lives and of those whom we have loved and who are now an unseen part of our mysterious universe. It has been said that life is being conscious and that death is only the unconscious part of life.

For those who do not find in themselves the idea of eternal life with the white clad angels enthralling, this revelation gives a man a new and surprising dignity: to walk tall, secure in the knowing that he is now in line and harmony with what men know of their world.

This age, which is the age of the Sage and Seer when wisdom replaces knowledge, is the time to find one's spiritual leader, to take a training, to accept a discipline, to ask all the questions and to know who the questioner really is. Who knows, perhaps the road to wisdom should start from the door of the Institute of Directors to Kathmandu or California, with ageing company men, backpacking on their way to discover themselves, carrying banners emblazoned with the words of George Bernard Shaw:

> This is the true joy of life, the being used a purpose recognised by yourself as a mighty one; the being a force of nature instead of a feverish, selfish little clod of ailments and grievances complaining that the world will not devote itself to making you happy.

> I want to be thoroughly used up when I die, for the harder I work the more I live, I rejoice in life for its own sake. Life is no 'brief candle' to me. It is a sort of splendid torch which I have got hold of for the moment, and I want to make burn as brightly as possible before handing it on to future generations.

These words are in fact the true essence of what growing old is and should be for all men. There are no limitations to the self, except those you believe in. For you and only you have is the creative energy that makes your world.

Commitment is the stuff character is
made of, the power to change the
face of things. It is the daily
triumph of integrity over scepticism.

And To the Least Of These

A man's reach should exceed his grasp or what's a Heaven for?

Robert Browning

This quotation is for me the very essence of what it means to be a World Runner, and whether you participated by running or supporting in the London Marathon, this was the truth you experienced, and in the reaching out you discovered that your limits were precisely those imposed on yourself by yourself.

You run for more than personal satisfaction, and well-being. In carrying the World Runner's message you add an extra motivation which improves the quality, commitment and the results of what you do, which is in itself no small bonus.

It is natural at some point that participants and supporters have doubts as to whether their running makes any contribution to the ending of hunger in the world. To what extent does carrying a message help? Would it not be better to have an organisation that would endorse and activate a development and get involved in the doing of it? Is this not the only satisfactory way?

We would be fools not to accept that people who are hungry now must be fed and the organisations that do that are worthy of all the support we can give; but having said that, the answer for many of us is still, no, it would not be better, for while we deal with the problems we must consider the solutions. With all the goodwill, love and charity that has gone into the world hunger problem over the last years, its persistence is greater than ever before. All the work that has been done to date appears to make no inroads.

It is then that we must ask ourselves why this should be so. What is the missing factor? What is the ingredient that is missing in all the plans that men have produced that allow hunger and starvation to persist in the world?

There is not one, but perhaps two hundred plans on ending world hunger and we do know that what is wanted is not more plans, but more men and women who believe that this is an idea whose time has come. When there are enough of us, then our leaders will decide that it is good politics to want to do something about it.

When this happens, whichever of the well-known solutions or combinations of them are appropriate will naturally be put into effect and will work.

WHAT IS MISSING, IS THE POLITICAL WILL TO MAKE IT HAPPEN.

Our forebears knew that the time had come for men, women and children to stand no longer in the market place in chains. It was no longer acceptable for men who called themselves civilised to bid for their fellow humans like cattle. It was when this became part of the consciousness of a nation and of our world that slavery ended.

It is the task of every successive generation to make its contributions to ongoing history, and the ending of hunger in the world is the contribution of those of us who are on our planet now. World Runners and the good news they carry are part of this contribution.

Running is our way of working this message into the awareness of the nation so that it eventually becomes part of the very fabric of our society. In London, in front of a million people, this is what we were doing.

What To Do Until The Undertaker Calls

To have entered the fourth lap of the race that is life with an awareness of this is to enter the Golden Age of man, is to join the few who see this period of life as an exciting challenge. For, if inwardly one appears to be of less use now, outwardly, one is a free spirit that can rise to new heights.

Could it be that its purpose now is for man to restate his belief in himself as planetary man, and to reject the doctrine of separateness? Could it be that in the two final decades of this century, mankind can come towards a greater realisation of his own unity? Could it be that those of us present now on this planet can give fuller expression to the idea of planetary man?

For in our lifetime we have seen just how fragile and vulnerable our planet is, how the sea-borne wastes of one continent become the marine pollution of some distant shore; how the toxic fumes of one industrial complex can fall as acid rain damaging forests hundreds of miles away. And the over-fishing in some Arctic Sea by one nation can imperil and destroy the industry and markets of another. Finally, in our lifetime we have seen the invention of nuclear weapons capable of destroying ourselves and our life support system. This should concentrate our minds.

Man and his environment are one; they cannot be separated, for we did not so much come into the world but out of it. Man is not an alien creature imposed on this planet. He is here as of right, as are the galaxies in the sky. He is the star in the heavens.

Separateness is the greatest illusion. It is what Einstein calls:

The delusion of consciousness, where we restrict our personal desire to a few persons nearest to us. The challenge is to free ourselves from this prison by widening our circle of compassion to embrace all living creatures, the whole nature in its beauty.

If this is too esoteric, too big a break with old beliefs that man is a tribal creature, the final lap has more attraction if we do no more than accept the view that we are young to ourselves and most of our lives young to our elders, as long as we have any. You look at the world with exactly the same eyes, eyes that say you are no older, only that you have been around longer. People are as much individuals at sixty-five, with different tastes, abilities, wants and needs, as they are at eighteen, and old is always fifteen years older than you are.

You find you not so much grew old, as less young, and have reached an age where you really get to choose... is life a tale told by an idiot, signifying nothing?... or is it that "splendid torch?"

If the idea of eternal life surrounded by white-clad angels has little appeal, you will not be the first to have lost 'hope of heaven' in the sense that your forefathers held it as a 'better place – somewhere up there'.

If you have little confidence in everlasting life, or indeed any great yearning for it, and you make the discovery that in the final lap of the race, the old beliefs were not so much replaced as transformed by the new awareness that it is the greatest of all privileges to be born a human being; and the search for understanding of the reality of the universe, the greatest undertaking which a person can involve himself.

But it is our tragedy that 'we live in a world without vision'. This is possibly the most dangerous situation in which human beings can find themselves. "Everything which works today began with a vision – a group of idealists prepared to work for it writes the late Barbara Ward. We learn from visionaries; we don't learn from practical men of affairs. They are good once the direction has been set. You do not find them in the forefront."

explains the late Barbara Ward

Our deepest fear is not that we are inadequate. Our deepest fear is that we are powerful beyond measure. It is our light, not our darkness, that most frightens us. We ask ourselves, 'who am I to be brilliant, gorgeous, talented, fabulous?'
Actually, who are you not to be? You are a child of God. Your playing small doesn't serve the world. There's nothing enlightened about shrinking so that other people won't feel insecure around you. We are all meant to shine, as children do... And as we let our own light shine, we unconsciously give other people permission to do the same. As we're liberated from our own fear, our presence automatically liberates others.

Nelson Mandela,
Inauguration Address as President of South Africa, 1994

Some reflections on

Mandela In America

and The Hunger Project Award

In the fall of 1979 my wife and I made our first visit to The Hunger Project's international office in San Francisco. The Hunger Project had proclaimed its commitment to:

1. the idea that ending hunger is 'an idea whose time has come'.

2. that hunger will end when hungry people are empowered to end their own hunger.

This was considered in those early days somewhat naïve.

That hunger should be ended, not just handled better or more efficiently, but ended once and for all and forever, was the vision of The Hunger Project and the unleashing of the human spirit for the end of hunger in the world was its global commitment.

For us the missing factor in the ending of hunger was the lack of political will to have it handled and to know that political will is created out of popular will, and creating that popular will was the point of entry into The Hunger Project for us both.

We worked with volunteers in an atmosphere of commitment and camaraderie the like of which I had only ever known before in wartime. Here were a group of fellow men and women, committed as in war to go beyond their limitations, every day doing more than would be reasonably expected and they delivered day after day. As in wartime, they were undaunted and this was heady stuff. It seemed to me that if war was the ultimate in a you OR me situation, then the war against the persistence of hunger in the world is the ultimate of a you AND me situation.

It was a war that called forth human beings to be heroic and they were. My own awareness was heightened by the experience. I had moved from operating out of charity to operating out of a sense of communion. This group I thought were living as men and women were meant to live and had created something very new for themselves. No longer doing more of the same, they had been pointed towards a star by which all our lives could now steer.

The experience that we had over these weeks, in this company, had touched me deeply and towards the end of our day I woke one morning at first light, quietly left the bedroom to avoid disturbing my wife and from the living room watched the dawn break across the bay.

On this particular morning I had an uncontrollable desire to put out on the wind some part of me, some wish to reach out to the six hundred million who awakened that day to hunger; in the still of the morning I opened the window, unconcerned by time or place, and called aloud:

"We are coming. Not leaders and followers but aligned together from many lands, shoulder to shoulder, too late to save you my little friend, but your brother and sister yet to be, for them we will be there, we will be there." Aware of a voice calling from the bedroom, are you all right, who are you talking to? I replied, "it is nothing, sorry I disturbed you." It was at this moment, at the closing of the window, that a clear and startling voice-like thought crying out came back on the wind.

"Wait! Wait one moment! Not MY brother and sister, YOUR brother and sister! For I am you and you are me and this is it."

It is some years since this experience and I have often questioned it. Many times I wondered if it was nothing more than a figment of the imagination, some hallucination, some trick of the wind. Yet, I cannot explain that when I doubt my own commitment, when I think that what I have done or said or given in this cause is enough, there is always this voice returning in my waking moments with the same message that brings me back to my purpose.

My reluctance until now to share this very private moment is explicable, if it was some cosmic experience, such experiences are more common than we might suppose. Polls indicate between a third and a half of the adult population in Britain and the U.S. would claim to be aware of or influenced by a presence or power whether they call it GOD or not, which is different from their everyday selves. If it came out of my own awareness, out of my own consciousness, if this was some moment in and out of time when it appeared that GOD was closer to me than I was to myself, then that moment needed to be protected. To protect it from the cynics, the ignorant and the mockers that make up some part of one's own acquaintance. I imagined the comment: "Have you heard? Waldron has got a touch of the Joan of Arc's. Do get him to tell you about his voices."

We live in a world where for many a vision is a joke, and only bread and butter realism, however dreary, is the only diet that can be tolerated. After all, hearing voices is dangerous stuff, as Joan of Arc would witness. One had no desire to be roasted alive by ridicule.

Yet I know now, it can be told, no one has to be convinced, sufficient it is to know that the moment was true for me. This is part of self-knowledge, to acquire the wisdom of discovering a clearer contact with an inner source, this intuition, creates a space in which you hear your own heartbeats and in that space your heart can speak with a voice that is mysteriously clear.

Fifteen years on, again the fall, again in America, this time not in the company of a handful of enthusiasts, but surrounded by a sea of faces of men and women with President Clinton present on the platform, who have come to honour Nelson Mandela, an exceptional man of his time, with the Africa Prize for Leadership for the Sustainable End of Hunger and a cheque for $100,000. This was the 8th year this prize has been awarded by The Hunger Project to leading Africans, women and men.

In his acceptance speech, President Mandela addressed us as brothers and sisters, echoing my voice from the past. His vision and commitment included a call for new income earning opportunities for his nation; the empowerment of women, for access to primary health care and education. There was more to his vision than rhetoric, for without such an agenda, without funding, it would, like any vision, remain only a pipe dream.

To fund your vision has always been both a primary objective and challenge for The Hunger Project.

We sat down to dinner, not a handful, but 1400 of us from all parts of the world, in an electric atmosphere in which the 'will to do good' was felt deeply and passed between men and women at every table. President Mandela in his address said:

"We do not want freedom without bread, nor do we want bread without freedom."

We felt the need to respond to this model of leadership which could inspire men and women to join the men and women of Africa in creating a new future.

When Joan Holmes, the president of The Hunger Project, presented the award she said, "that President Mandela's agenda to ensure every child, woman and man, has the opportunity to live a healthy and productive life was an agenda for the ending of hunger."

For some of us of the old guard, this was more than an award dinner, it was a validation, it was an act of renewal. We reached out and found in each other a strengthened commitment to play our part with the people of Africa in creating the future that Mandela had visualised and inspired.

More powerful than a thousand armies
is an idea whose time has come.

Victor Hugo

This extract is from:

THE AQUARIAN CONSPIRACY
by Marilyn Ferguson
pages 412 to 416
and present a view of

THE HUNGER PROJECT

It should be essential reading for volunteers.

This brilliant book is now available in hardback and paperback

1. The Aquarian Conspiracy

Little by little, those who undertake the transformative process discern the existence of a vast support network.

"It's a lonely path," one of the conspirators said, "but you aren't alone in it." The network is more than a mere association of like-minded persons. It offers moral support, feedback, an opportunity for mutual discovery and reinforcement, ease, intimacy, celebration, a chance to share experiences and pieces of the puzzle.

Erich Fromm's blueprint for social transformation emphasised the need for mutual support, especially in small groups of friends: "Human solidarity is the necessary condition for the unfolding of any one individual." "No transformation, no supermind, without such friends," said the narrator of Michael Murphy's novel, *Jacob Atabet*, based in part on the experiments and explorations of Murphy and his friends. "We are midwives to each other."

The immense fulfilment of the friendships between those engaged in furthering the evolution of consciousness has a quality impossible to describe, Teilhard once said. Barbara Marx Hubbard called the intense affinity "supra-sex" – an almost sensual longing for communion with others who have the larger vision. Psychologist Jean Houston wryly called it "swarming", and one conspirator spoke of "the network as fraternity".

There is a conspiracy to make it less risky for people to experience transformation, said a 1978 letter from John Denver, Werner Erhard and Robert Fuller, past president of Oberlin College.

Acknowledging to ourselves and to you that we are all members of this 'conspiracy' to make the world a safer place for personal and social transformation brings us clarity of purpose and a sense of relatedness as we go about our business.

In fact, the original meaning of conspiracy is to 'breathe together', which expresses exactly what we have in mind. We are together.

2. Ending Hunger – Creating a Paradigm Shift

Historically, movements for social change have all operated in much the same way. A paternal leadership has convinced people of the need for change, then recruited them for specific tasks, telling them what to do and when to do it. The new social movements operate on a different assumption of human potential: the belief that individuals once they are deeply convinced of a need for change, can generate solutions from their own commitment and creativity. The larger movement inspires them, it supports their efforts and gives them information, but its structure cannot direct or contain their efforts.

The power of individuals to generate broad social change is the basis for The Hunger Project. The Hunger Project's goal is to speed up a solution to the world hunger problem by acting as a catalyst. It is an intense, sophisticated large-scale effort to hurry a paradigm shift – "to make an idea's time come", as the projects organisers put it. The successes of the project and the ways in which it has been misunderstood are instructive.

The Hunger Project assumes that solutions do not reside in new programs or more programs. According to the best informed authorities and agencies, the expertise to end hunger within two decades already exists. Hunger persists because of the old-paradigm assumption that it is not possible to feed the world's population.

To create a sense of urgency, the project draws on the power of the symbol and the metaphor, describing the toll of starvation as "a Hiroshima every three days." When a Hunger Project relay of more than one thousand runners carried a baton from Maine to the White House, they did not ask the government to solve the problem. Rather, their message spoke of their own commitment to help end hunger and starvation.

The project uses models from nature and scientific discoveries as metaphors; the hologram, for example, is "a whole within a whole". Everyone who enrols is "the whole project". The project is "an alignment of wholes". Everyone who signs up is told to "create your own form of participation." Some fast and contribute to the project what they would have spent on food. Many businesses have donated a day's receipts. A team of forty runners generated pledges of six hundred and twenty-five thousand dollars for running in the Boston Marathon in 1979, and twenty three hundred spectators were enrolled along the way. Eighty-eight fifth graders in a California school sponsored a Skate-a-thon and raised six hundred dollars; when they designated their funds for 'the boat people', the Hunger Project put them in touch with Food for the Hungry, an organisation directly assisting the refugees.

Everyone who signs up is encouraged to enlist others. Enrolees are told how to capture the interest of clubs, school boards, lawmakers; how to direct letters; how to make public presentations. Each enrolee is asked to become a teacher. Seminars emphasise the power of a single committed person, like the man in New Rochelle, New York, who enrolled his mayor, school superintendent, city manager, governor, and lieutenant governor; and the Honolulu woman who signed up the entire congressional delegation, governor, and most of the state legislature. At her urging, the governor proclaimed Hunger Week, and state legislators passed a resolution to encourage Hawaiian agricultural research to help alleviate world hunger. A Massachusetts couple enrolled fifty thousand.

Within a year after the launching of the project, ninety committees had been organised in thirteen countries. Celebrities spoke out for the cause, sometimes without specific reference to the project, much as movie stars helped sell war bonds in the 1940s. Singer John Denver made a documentary film on world hunger. He told a newspaper interviewer:

"We're at a point in this planet where we're going to have to make a specific shift in attitude, in how we lend ourselves to life. Up until now it's been: 'If this were the last cup of grain, my very survival depends on my keeping it for me and my own.' Now we're at a time when we will shift to: my survival depends on my sharing this with you. If this isn't enough for me, my survival still depends on my sharing this with you."

Denver, now on the Presidential Commission on World Hunger, wrote, "I Want To Live", the title song on a gold-record album, for the Hunger Project. Its theme: We are on the threshold of the end of war and starvation. "It is only an idea – but I know its time has come."

A key point is made to those who sign up: a world in which hunger has ended will be not merely different or better but transformed. And those who take part will be transformed by their own participation – by telling friends, family, and co-workers of their own commitment, even if they feel self-conscious, and by searching for answers.

3. Re-choosing

Over the centuries those who envisioned a transformed society knew that relatively few shared their vision. Like Moses, they felt the breezes from a homeland they could see in the distance but not inhabit. Yet they urged others on to the possible future. Their dreams are our rich, unrealised history, the legacy that has always existed alongside our wars and folly.

In a wider state of consciousness one can sometimes vividly re-experience a past trauma and, in retrospect and with imagination, respond to it differently. By thus touching the source of old fear, we can exorcise it. We are not haunted so much by events as by our beliefs about them, the crippling self-image we take with us. We can transform the present and future by re-awakening the powerful past, with its recurrent message of defeat. We can face the crossroads again. We can re-choose.

In a similar spirit, we can respond differently to the tragedies of modern history. Our past is not our potential. In any hour, with all the stubborn teachers and healers of history who called us to our best selves, we can liberate the future. One by one, we can re-choose – to awaken. To leave the prison of our conditioning, to love, to turn homeward. To conspire with and for each other.

Awakening brings its own assignments, unique to each of us, chosen by each of us. Whatever you may think about yourself, and however long you may have thought it, you are not just you. You are a seed, a silent promise. You are the conspiracy.

with acknowledgement and thanks
to Marylin Ferguson and her
publishers for permission to reprint
this extract

Hunger And The Bomb

Hiroshima 40th Anniversary Lecture

delivered by
Victor E. Waldron

at the Salisbury Medical Centre
Salisbury Infirmary, Wiltshire
on 6th August 1985
and sponsored by
The Medical Campaign Against Nuclear Weapons

Author's Note

It is not a contradiction to believe as increasing numbers do:

1. That the use of the nuclear bomb is not an option to be considered, however dire the circumstances.

2. If a nation insists in giving first priority to 'defence' expenditure, this should not be allowed to defer the allocation of adequate resources for the ending of world hunger. The developed world is rich enough to afford both and it is not a case of either/or.

This is the view of my Quaker friend Walter Birmingham, to whom I dedicate this pamphlet and whose book *How much more?* started me down this road.

The Hiroshima Lecture

16 August 1985

It was three years ago that I contributed some part to the formation of a Business Industry Forum for International Stability. The Forum's inaugural meeting at the Royal Society for Medicine was privileged to have a prominent member of the medical profession, Professor Sir Richard Doll, to give the keynote address.

The opening remarks on that occasion made by Sir Richard Doll are so appropriate to our meeting here tonight that I would like to read them to you. He said:

> I do wish to tell you of an experience I had a month ago when visiting Nagasaki for the first time while on a lecture tour of Japan. I was the guest of Dr Michito Ecimura, a Professor of Nagasaki University. Dr Ecimaru was a medical student in 1945 and on the 9th of August 1945 he went to school in the normal way, but when he got to his tram stop, he found there had been a derailment and the trams would not be running for two hours. He decided to go home and study there, an hour later a bomb was dropped about two hundred yards from the medical school. He went to the school and found every single medical student, even teachers, either dead or dying. You can imagine what it must have been like trying to pull dying colleagues from the debris. Dr Ecimaru is now an active member of the International Physicians for the Prevention of Nuclear War. Meeting him made such an impression on me that I felt I would like to start this meeting by relating his experience and remind you that the bomb had only about one thousandth of the power of current bombs, of which there are many thousands in existence.

Tonight, forty years on, we meet in another medical school, knowing that whatever the advances of medical science, man himself has advanced but little. We, with millions of others, for the first time in human history are concerned about ourselves, our children, and are deeply anxious about our world and its future. It is a terrifying situation that in any future we should have, our right to live should depend on a small group of people in two capitals of the world, over whose actions we here have no influence, no control and no vote.

The Medical Campaign Against Nuclear Weapons formed in the UK in 1980 as an association of doctors and health care workers who are united in the belief that nuclear war <u>is not an option that should ever be allowed to be considered against any nation, however dire the circumstances</u>.

You understand the medical consequences of a nuclear war, you know what it is to have an ethical responsibility for the health of patients, and above all you have strong international links and you are used to dealing with problems that transcend national boundaries.

Both your associations are affiliated to the International Physicians for Prevention of Nuclear War, that now has a membership of 100,000 in fifty-three countries. So both as a profession and as individuals yours is a considerable contribution and I am very conscious of the privilege afforded me in talking to you this evening.

When Dr Mark Podkolinski asked me to do this lecture, I had some apprehensions. It is a privilege to speak to men of your skill and learning and I looked at my own life without any particular academic background and wondered what message I would have for you, out of my own experience. I found it challenging to attempt a contribution that did more that reiterate the anti-nuclear arguments, most of which would be familiar to you.

It was Robert McNamara in his valedictory speech when he left the World Bank who said that in the final analysis, the issue of world hunger (and I think this true of war) was not going to be solved by technicians, experts, scientists, but it would be solved by caring people. It seems to me, that is a statement of who we all are, and for the next hour or so we are in the right place.

Looking back on this long journey, there are some meaningful moments which give me the position from which I can comment to some purpose. The first 'Y' junction I faced on this road was the realisation that it is only in the last five years that my preoccupation with making a living became secondary to a decision that I spend the rest of my days doing more and more of the same until I reached the end of allotted span was not the essence of personal fulfilment, somewhere 'out there' issues which, if you were to have your life make a difference (to me the doctrine that you can't make a difference is pernicious and soul destroying), are issued which were urgent and required a commitment that would generate action.

The experience of businessmen who wait six months for a letter to be answered is that Soviet Marxism is a top-heavy, cumbersome bureaucracy, and is as out of place in the age of high tech as a gear shift on a computer. Many hold the view that one of the things that prevents any change in the system is the fierceness of the USA opposition to it and the knowledge that to do so would be misinterpreted as weakness.

In four days time, I shall be in Moscow. I was last in Russia during the war as RNVR Officer, serving in what was euphemistically called a Defensively Equipped Merchant Ship. It will be my first visit to the capital and it will be interesting to see to what extent, if any, this view required modification.

It is forty years since I was with our ex-allies-companions-in-arms, who faced three-quarters of the German strength and defeated it; a fact which puts our own victory into perspective and who we are now asked to see as 'our mortal enemy'.

Contrary to what is often said in the West, looking for a way to co-exist does not necessarily mean changing the foundation of their system even if we had the power to do so.

May I turn to another speech at another anniversary of forty years ago and quote another man's words? He said:

"The responsibility of great states is to serve and not dominate people of the world. We can no longer permit any nation or group of nations to settle their arguments with bombs."

Forty years ago these were the words of President Truman as he opened the inaugural meeting of the United Nations at San Francisco and it echoed the hopes and the dreams, the visions of all of those who had served through the war, and was America expressing herself at her greatest, giving inspired leadership to the world.

The great danger is that the United States is the world's dominant economic power, if it decides to maintain high military spending and chooses not to pay for it out of domestic taxation, but out of foreign borrowing, the perverse result will be that the whole world suffers from a regime of high interest rates that follow and the poorest and most heavily indebted countries are the ones who pay most.

Major powers argue that the nuclear deterrent strategy has succeeded in keeping the peace for forty years. It is a hard one to answer, yet the proposition that if our children are to inherit the earth we must have the capacity to destroy it several times over is assuredly losing credibility.

The situation becomes more obscene with the new dimension in military spending, when the Star Wars program is considered, it is in Shidrath Ramphal's words like having a medical research program to ensure eternal life. "How long," he asked, "would it take those who place reliance on new militarisation of outer space (rather than limitation of arms) before it leads to major policy changes, policies for securing peace through preparing for war. This is half-way to guaranteeing security by a war to end wars, a call that our fathers answered in 1914 to no avail. We are being prepared," said Shidrath Ramphal, "for a collective jump from the 'frying pan into the fire.'"

It is tragic that the military way of thinking is not confined to the military powers for our contribution as armament salesmen extends well into the Third World. They too have allowed themselves to acquire major modern weapons as symbols of progress or props for their political power. It is a staggering fact that we have had 130 armed conflicts in ninety countries on various scales in the three decades since the end of the Second World War.

The four horsemen of the Apocalypse are riding and if one is war then hard on his heels are his companions: famine, pestilence and hunger. Willy Brandt, when heading the Brandt Commission, said that, "while most recognise that one of the aftermaths of war is hunger and famine, history shows it is less recognised that hunger and famine can be the cause of war." It is Brandt who expresses the view that while hunger rules peace will not prevail. Morally, he said, it matters little if a human being dies in war or is condemned to starve to death because of the indifference of others.

He who would ban war must first ban hunger, for hunger in the last five years has killed more than all the wars in the last 150 years.

"More arms do not make man safer, only poorer," says the Brandt Commission, "and the poor must be provided with the conditions by which they can be saved from starvation as well as destructive confrontation."

The possibility of this destructive confrontation is being increasingly recognised as the flash-point of a nuclear war. War is far more likely to start in one of the unstable economies of the Third World than from eyeball-to-eyeball confrontation between the super powers. The unstable countries are the danger points, the trigger points, whether in South America, Central America, the Middle East, they are the battle fronts in which smaller nations, encouraged by the sponsorship of one or other of the two super powers, are the most likely areas for a confrontation that could turn into world conflict.

Brandt makes clear that to bring stability to these economies is now a matter of self-interest, and if the moral arguments have failed to move men, self-interest must surely have its turn.

It is not diminishing the importance of the nuclear debate to say that it is also the great 'IF' debate of our time. If we take a multi-lateral view, if we take the unilateral view, if missiles are stored, in this or that place, or if the bomb drops. Each 'IF' engenders a counter-argument and each counter-argument pours forth its own extra rebuttal as a conditioned reflex. Each is held by men in good faith. The other debate has been pinpointed by Willy Brandt with his statement that hunger kills at the rate of three Hiroshima bombs a week. There is no IF about it. That is for real; that is the truth this week, next week and the week after.

We must remember that with all the millions of words that have been used on this subject and all the millions yet to come, 75% of the world's population are bored by the bomb. Voices from Africa and Latin America would dismiss it as a toy problem, merely hypothetical agony, while the problems of famine and disease are near and urgent.

Six hundred million awake each day to hunger, and that is not just their problem, but our problem too. Five years ago that fact was less easily heard, (it seemed a strange truth when I first heard it), but today there are ever-increasing numbers of people who not only know this as a truth, but live out their lives as if they know it.

Those who are hungry now must be fed now. They cannot live on theories, and if I have said little of the work of the charities and the aid agencies, it is not out of indifference. I believe that our debt to the organisations that do this work is immeasurable. My experience of them, from the great household names such as Oxfam, Christian Aid, and Save the Children, to the many smaller ones, is that they are manned in the field by men and women of great compassion and understanding and their administrators at home are men and women of great ability and deep commitment.

My gratitude for eighty years in which I have never known what it is to be hungry, even for one day, makes the face of the starving Ethiopian child a haunting one. I believe him worthy of more than my charity, and on the question of entitlement he has both right and justice on his side.

I have learned that whatever my own achievements, whatever the achievements of our world, whatever the breakthroughs we have had in medicine, in science, in industry, these are down-graded and we are diminished by the fact that they are made in a world where children in their millions are expected to starve to death.

Both the hunger and the nuclear issues have the 'sound barrier' of indifference to break through. It sometimes seems that the vested interest of those who appear to want the world to stay as it is are unbeatable. Left of Right, the forces for the status quo are powerful. End World Capitalism. This trivialises the issue, it is a strange commentary that the more it is shown that unbridled socialism has done little to improve the condition of world hunger, those on the Left answer, bigger and bigger doses of the same. On the other side of the coin you find as much evidence that market forces are painfully inadequate and unhelpful, yet with equal dedication the operation of uninhibited market forces is the only requirement that will bring a solution.

Whatever the ideology, the case of the starving is unassailable, but neither Left nor Right are ready to rethink and restructure aid, nor are they ready to increase the incentives for Third World producers to become self-reliant or to foster the political and economic condition to make this possible.

As Maurice Strong noted at the SID World Conference:

"The Western media have tended to create the false impression that these people are not doing enough for themselves and that they have been receiving foreign aid for years. So what must be wrong with them?"

As Strong emphasised, "most of the people affected by the drought and famine in Africa are people who have never received assistance from their own government, let alone from foreigners. They never expected anything, they have never received anything, and this is 95% of them". He added, "they are tough-minded, dignified, self-reliant people and it has taken four and sometimes five years of successive droughts really to force them to go where perhaps they find a little food for their families."

"The landless peasant," said Werner Erhard, "required more courage to rise and face his day followed by the eyes of his hungry wife and children than many of us are called upon to display in our lifetimes."

The need for a vision in our lives and in our nation is urgent. We need to have our vision expressed as a global strategy; political, social, economic, based on a reverence for life, a vision of a world which will work, not just for some, but for all men.

To work, to plan, and to fund, for to involve yourself in it is to involve yourself in your own fulfilment. In the words of William James, "A man's vision is the great fact about him."

I believe that the issues, whether they are hunger or war, are philosophical as well as political. I believe in the necessity of proclaiming a view of man as more than a consumer and more than an appetite.

Politically what is obvious to us all is that neither a Socialist Paradise nor a Capitalist Utopia can be built on a mountain of corpses; that the destiny of man is to finish under the stairs in his D.I.Y. nuclear shelter made from two old doors and two brown paper bags according to the latest Government directives.

Philosophically, it has been said by cleverer men than me that 'whatever you may think about yourself, and however long you may have thought it, you are more than just you, you are a seed, a silent promise, a free spirit.' Although it is in the very nature of man to lose sight of his own uniqueness and to disbelieve in his own greatness, this remains a truth.

The Three Phases

Historically, any movement that advances a cause from a new direction goes through three phases:

1. Ridicule/Criticism

2. Argument/Discussion

3. Adoption/Acceptance

One hopes that criticism from the media, when it comes, will be truthful and acceptable. If it is not, a young organisation must assess how much time and effort it should spend refuting such attacks and what will be the cost to itself if it is side-tracked from its own true purpose. If the decision was made to defend the truth, what would we find?

First, the press, in the words of *The Wall Street Journal* now:

> sees its major function as 'making news!' not reporting it objectively. It has created a new journalism, a sensationalism, a desire for scandal, controversy, excitement, titillation and above all the destruction of reputations.

This is all part and parcel of its daily fare. Whether it is true, half true or false, is beside the point to any so called 'Investigative Journalist': there is only 'news to be made'.

What does the media itself say of this new journalism? The magazine *Cosmopolitan*, in an article in August:

> If sinister poison pens are to be the new accolade of merit for Fleet Street success,
>
> the truth of the evidence is being used as much as a dog uses a lamp-post.

No wonder that more and more newspaper readers would turn first and more often than not last, to the sports pages, where athletes make news, not journalists.

Edward Heath's article on the Brandt Commission for Shift in the Wind which goes to one and a half million households, making it the widest circulating newspaper in the world on the subject of World Hunger, was produced at a time when Brandt and the work of the Commission had made little or no impact in America and it was a powerful contribution to USA understanding.

When the Hunger Project celebrated its 2,000,000th enrolment in the Palace of Fine Arts in San Francisco in 1982, 1,000 people listened to messages from world leaders.

Willy Brandt wrote:

I am greatly encouraged by your efforts. The fact of millions of starving people cannot leave us indifferent. I encouraged you to continue your endeavours and I wish you every success.

The message from the Archbishop of Canterbury was prefixed with the opening words:

Your conference is a message of hope in a world where hope is in short supply.

All this world-wide acknowledgement of the work of The Hunger Project is, not, as one press article:

That if enough people will hunger to end then the problem will go away.

This impression of the Hunger Project enrolees sitting around cross-legged in the middle of the floor studying their navels and willing hunger to go away, must rate as a most destructive and irresponsible piece of mischief.

The Hunger Project, believes that individuals, once they are deeply convinced of a need for change, can generate solutions from their own commitment and creativity. Your paternalist can direct and inform; he cannot inspire or contain the effort. It is said that Marx, towards the end of his life, declared that he was not a Marxist. There is little doubt that a returning Christ would have some problems.

That the criticism of the Hunger Project as 'American orientated' leads one to spell out to them, that like it or not, if the world is ever to be a morally habitable place, it will contain one or two Americans.

Left or right, the forces for the status quo are powerful. End World Hunger for the left is converted to the slogan End World Capitalism. This trivialises the issue and it is a strange commentary the more it is shown that unbridled socialism has done little to improve the condition of world hunger. Those on the left have only one answer and that is for bigger and bigger doses of the same. On the other side of the coin you find as much evidence that market forces are painfully unhelpful, yet they, with equal dedication, advance the theory that the freeing of the market, the operation of uninhibited market forces is the only requirement that will bring a solution.

The reaction of our business friends to all this is often one of alarm. They wish to be left alone. Their favourite argument is:

> Let us get on with our jobs; let us make
> our profit. Eventually, the benefits will
> trickle down to the poor and needy.

The 'trickle-down' theory has had its followers. Others see their world as a lifeboat in which we are safely on board, now loaded down to the gunwales. However much they sympathise with those men, women and children who are swimming around out there with little hope of survival, any suggestion that we could pull them on board is dangerously stupid and can only result in drowning us all.

The Queen's Christmas Broadcast (usually non-controversial), daringly suggested that we need a little less nationalism and a little more 'sense of our interdependence' with the rest of the world. This was sufficient for the *Times* to write leaders expressing strong disapproval and to continue the criticism over a period of three months.

All these assumptions are equally spurious, and the analogy is unhelpful and untrue. Planetary man is in the only boat there is available for us all, spaceship earth, and those travelling steerage are in dire straits, with a leaking hull, stinking bilges and unworkable pumps, and it is foolish for those of us who are on the upper deck to spend our time drinking beef tea and putting out the deck chairs.

When the going is at its toughest and those with a vested interest in having the world stay as it is are at their loudest, the truth of Goethe's words becomes apparent:

> The moment one commits oneself, then Providence moves too, all sorts of things occur to help one that would never have otherwise occurred. A whole stream of events issued from the decision, raising in one's favour all manner of unforeseen incidents, that no man would have dreamed of coming his way.

The truth of this was shown by the two events which have rapidly followed each other. First, who could have conceived that Oxfam would suddenly appear with a new program 'Hungry for Change' to which they commit themselves to arouse the public conscience, a field in which we have operated as the pathfinders for so long. This new campaign to create awareness means that the Consciousness-Raising Lobby is about to have a million pound injection of Oxfam money and The Hunger Project's response is 'Welcome Aboard'.

If it is from the Hunger Project that many first understood that one quarter of our world is hungry and that it is not 'their problem' but 'our problem'. If that fact is acceptable now to more and more people, it was a strange truth in the ears of many in 1977. 'Not their problem, but our problem', was an expression of man's humanity to have an increasing number of people not just know this truth, but live out their lives as if they know it.

Secondly, it is appropriate that on World Food Day, October 16th, comes the information from the Charity Commission that having satisfied their searching inquiries, the Hunger Project is granted charitable status in the United Kingdom.

We have had the criticism and the argument.

We have reached Phase Three – acceptance and adoption.

The Hunger Project is developing independently in many countries, each from the perspective of their own culture, each celebrating their own achievements and correcting their own mistakes. The critics will come and the critics will go, but the inspiration of the men and women – and one person in particular, who first sourced the ending of hunger, as an idea whose time has come, will remain. It was of such that William James spoke when he said "a man's vision is the great fact about him."

THE  TIMES

THURSDAY APRIL 13 1989

NEWS ROUNDUP

Charity wins damages

Times Newspapers agreed yesterday to pay undisclosed damages to each of eight trustees of the Hunger Project Trust and legal costs after an article in *The Sunday Times* suggested the charity was a front for something which the newspaper described as a Californian sect. The attacks had a serious effect on the charity's good name and the reputation of trustees, Mr Andrew Monson, for the trust, told Mr Justice Brooke in the High Court, London. Mr Geoffrey Shaw, for Times Newspapers, said it regretted publishing damaging falsehoods and innuendoes and apologized for the embarrassment and distress caused.

We Meet The Press

He that steals my purse steals trash,
'tis something – nothing, 'tis mine 'tis his
and has been slave to thousands.
But, he that filches from me my good name,
takes that which in no way enriches him
But leaves me poor – indeed.

William Shakespeare

In the years in which Olivia and I were most active in the work of The Hunger Project, the year 1989 was the most traumatic. We had been aware of what we called the abstractions and that men might misconstrue them. When it happened we faced the task and we accepted the challenge.

The Hunger Project articles of Association quite clearly put the objects into focus, and so guaranteed the granting of charitable status. That hunger should be ended once and for all and forever and the lack of political will to have it handled was the missing factor. Our inability so far to create the political will to have it handled was the priority for us who were involved. Creating the political will was the object to which we gave our money, our time and our skills.

The shock when Andrew Neil of *The Sunday Times* with all the weight of a major Murdoch newspaper, presented this as not only a scam but an American one and not only American but Californian, made it in his view, "a strange cult".

That the directors were libelled after giving so much and to find that the answer would require nothing less than a High Court action with all the commitments of gigantic legal costs was a chastening thought.

With the money and the power and machinery at their command they had a vested interest in keeping the negotiations at an arms length.

Our commitment was to see justice done and the awareness that our costs were now close to £200,000 left one asking were we rushing in where angels fear to tread. To this was added the similar costs of the other side which meant that if a decision went against us, the eight directors involved would be represented with the financial disaster.

We learned that the old adage 'that British justice was open to everyone, just like the Ritz Hotel' was a truism.

The Hunger Project's statement that hunger is not inevitable and it can be ended and that individuals have this within their grasp was restated by none other than 79 Nobel Laureates who, signed the manifesto against hunger, who finished with a statement that putting an end to hunger is a reasonable and achievable goal.

This fact, while of great concern to us, was known to *The Sunday Times*, who could well afford to take the problem of costs in their stride.

The cat and mouse game continued, and only in the morning that the case was to come to Court did the legal representatives of the Murdoch newspapers come forward with an acceptable apology on terms agreeable to us.

This statement made in the High Court of Justice by *The Sunday Times* regretted publishing damaging falsehoods and innuendoes and apologised for the embarrassment and distress caused, agreed to pay all our costs plus a sum to each director. The apology published in *The Times* of Thursday April 13, 1989, although regrettably not on the front page, coincided with our wedding anniversary and gave an added cause for celebration.

MORE LAST WORDS

Develop A Reputation For Charm

Charm is everything. It is a gift of nature and owes little to schooling, to which, in fact, it is superior. It is the life of the talents, the flower of speech, the soul of action, the halo of splendour itself. It is the simplest weapon, yet the most potent. It is a thing of ease, yet approaches daring; it takes the difficulty out of conversation and adds perfection to performance. Without charm, beauty is meaningless, and all grace, graceless, for this formidable trait transcends courage, wisdom, reason, and greatness itself. Charm is the courteous way to get about in every enterprise, and the polite way to wriggle out of every embarrassment.

Basac Jusvot
Died 1647

Her Ladyship's Man

"Explain to me," challenged my American friend, "if you can, some of the vagaries and oddities of the British aristocracy." Heaven only knows where to start! And heaven is not talking, I thought.

"Primogeniture, " I explained, the word coming to the rescue from some dark recess of my mind, "that is the inheritance of the firstborn; this has been a prime factor in the survival of the old aristocratic families. The eldest son inherits the entailed estate, the total investments, the land, the mansions, down to the last fittings.

The firstborn son inherits, the second son goes into the army, the next into the church, and should any others finish up in 'trade' this was not considered a suitable activity for the 'quality'. The quality, a good class-conscious expression, you find in the works of Jane Austin, Trollope and the Brontës. The British aristocracy improved on primogenitor by insisting on 'male primogenitor'. By modern standards this seems extremely unfair to ignore the females, and in this age of sexual equality it still survives. However unfair, keeping the family fortune together rather than dividing it among large families has proved the salvation of many aristocratic generations.

"Now," said my friend, "how does this work or affect everyday life?" Let me tell you a story of how it affected me, was my reply.

My wife, as you know, has a courtesy title, which she retained when she married me, a commoner, and we lived for some years at Windsor in the shadow of the Royal castle. Among the tradesmen there was a certain amount of "Yes, M'Lady, No, M'Lady," and the touching of forelocks.

"You will be in Windsor with the children" said my wife. "Please call in to the butcher and collect the weekend joint I ordered." I dutifully presented myself to the butcher:

"Good morning, I have come to collect our joint."

"What name sir?" he asked.

"Waldron," I replied. This was followed by a call to his assistant in the nether regions of the shop.

"Lord Waldron calling for Her Ladyship's leg! (of lamb). At this, my children, aged about seven and eight, fell about laughing and the perplexed butcher said, "Why the laughter sir? Have I said something wrong?"

"They are, I am afraid, highly amused at hearing me called Lord Waldron, which I am surely not." He was now extremely put out by the children's laughter, and turned, eyeing me up and down with some hostility and said:

"I suppose you are Her Ladyship's man?"

I like it! I repeated it again to myself! Her Ladyship's man! That is as a good a title as any to live by, bestowed upon me by the worthy butcher!

Within a few months we approach our fortieth anniversary, and if I ever find the time to write my reminiscences of those years, the butcher's title, conferred on me so many years ago, is the natural heading.

Morning Verse

Hot against my lips you lie,
Alone you are with me.
For you in bed each dawn I sigh,
Oh, morning cup of tea.

Anon

Where Elephants Sometimes Roam.

An Episode In The Life Of An English Village

It was not altogether to everyone's liking when in this delightful Berkshire country village a desirable property with agricultural land was purchased by Billy Smart's Circus as his winter quarters. Like it or not, we were to learn to live with the zebra, the elephant and the roaring lion at feeding time, and the raucous circus staff in our little country pub at drinking time.

The elephants were exercised by walking the country lanes, supervised by staff, head to tail, single file, in orderly manner, a sight which delighted the children, which became commonplace to us locals, but eye-popping to any motorist driving through the village for the first time.

On this occasion, a curious observer pulled up in front of the procession, which had been halted momentarily by the keeper at the side of the road. He was driving a small three wheeler car, popular after the war, a useful red run-about, little more than a single cockpit on wheels which you got into as if you were a fighter pilot, not inappropriate for the vehicle was produced by the famous German Messerschmidt company, who a few years earlier had produced the fighter planes that had crossed the skies over our heads.

To the utter surprise of the watchers and circus staff, the leading elephant quietly left his mates, walked up to the red bubble car so reminiscent of the bright tub on which he was accustomed to sit in the circus ring and sat firmly, with his full weight on the hood. The great beast somewhat shamefacedly, was persuaded to move, and the front of the little vehicle was well and truly stoved in. The sight of this huge creature sitting sedately in the middle of the road was really quite comic, unless of course you were the owner of the bubble car. After the usual exchange of insurance numbers and details, witnesses if any, the damage was such that the car was still fit to drive home.

Now was to develop the final indignity in one of those mornings when nothing seems to go right. A few miles away, at a busy crossroads and seconds before his arrival – a sudden emergency, a car braking, a multiple pile up as one after another half a dozen cars crashed into one another, resulting in casualties, police, ambulances, paramedics, all were to swing into action, an all too common sight these days.

He was coming from the opposite direction and not involved, but witnessing the pile up, he felt duty bound to pull over and render what assistance he could before the police arrived.

You can imagine the final scene, the casualties removed, the ambulances driven off, the wreckage removed, and the backlog of traffic beginning to clear. The police inspector came over to the bubble car to thank the driver for his help and noted his damaged car, and said, "You had better give my man the details of your damage, Sir."

"Oh no, Inspector, I was not involved, my damage was done by an elephant sitting on the hood." After a silence, the Inspector asked incredulously,

"An elephant, Sir? When was that Sir?" The reply came,

"In Crouch Lane an hour ago." He called over the paramedic.

"Are you sure you did not hit your head, Sir, let us have a look."

"No, no, it really was an elephant," protested the driver. By now a small group had joined, including the police doctor who took over the questioning.

"You say an elephant, Sir, in Crouch Lane, and what was the elephant doing?" The reply came,

"He was out walking with his mates, each held the tail of the one in front, if the one in front stopped they had sufficient distance to stop without a pile up, which was quite bright of them."

"I really do think," said the doctor, "you should go in the ambulance, you should let us give you a check over. At least sit down and let me look at you." He was now convinced he had a case of bad concussion, with hallucinations following a head injury, and the longer the explanations the more disbelief was generated.

This story is now part of the local pub folklore, re-told, embellished with the final interrogation by the wife, "Why two hours late for lunch? Why were you chatting to an elephant? Why did your Good Samaritan act lead to doubts as to your sanity? Why did the police insist they would only release you as fit to drive after a medical examination?"

The elephant may not remember any of this, but, for the driver, this was a Sunday morning he would never forget, and that's for sure.

Nightmare

Or By The Skin Of My Teeth

I was sixteen and a senior scouter in my local Sea Scout Troop. I took the group boat without authority, without qualification, out into the lower reaches of the river Thames, out in to the fairway, avoiding the sea going traffic, past the industrial wharves and jetties.

The boat, a 27 ft ex-naval whaler, usually rowed by five men, now had two boys to each bench to handle the heavy oars. My complement was twelve in all, very young, eleven to twelve years, on whom I intended to demonstrate my skills as a boat handler.

This unofficial, unauthorised voyage went well with the help of the fast running flood tide. My intention was that after two or three hours upstream, when the tide turned, we would row back to our base in the safety of the creek.

Now with supreme overconfidence and to the delight of the young rowers I decided to unship the mast, step it up into position, shake out a sail and beat for home with a fair wind.

My inexperience in sailboat handling led me to attempt to sail through the Barge Roads into the clear water beyond before coming about. The Barge Roads stretch for a mile, rows of 100 ton empty barges, moored in fours, usually seen being towed by a powerful tug, six at a time. This was the main mooring on the London river, resembling a giant railway siding on water.

As any sailboat man would have foreseen, the obvious happened, once between the barges the wind was blanketed from the sails, the helpless boat was carried by the racing tide on to a barge, under the projecting brow with a frightening crash.

The boat caught by the racing tide, jammed. firmly broadside on under the overhanging prow, nearly gunwale under and slowly tipping over, the scene was set for a major disaster. The stern was still free and from my position as the tallest and strongest I saw I could leap for a handhold onto the barge deck above me, then from a prone position I was able to grasp the hands of the smallest boys as they were passed up and climbed over me, making of me a human ladder to safety. The first ones, by sitting and holding onto my feet allowed me to stretch out further and grasp each boy in turn until all had reached the safety of the barge deck.

The boat now lightened, was no longer at such a frightening angle and we watched over the next two hours, first in horror, then in relief, as the tide slackened. The vice-like grip was now reversed and the boat floated free. We moored her alongside the barge, unshipped the mast and sail, and re-manned the boat. Helped by the ebb tide, we were a chastened and fairly silent crew as we rowed back to base, and moored in the correct, seamanlike manner. There the boys went home to mum, two hours late for tea and for the most part, unaware how close they had been to a watery grave.

But for me, sixty years on, the nightmare was always the same. As I aged the characters grew from boys to men, from men to officers. Always a Court Martial, the prosecuting counsel, the searching questions. "I suggest, Waldron, that in leaping and abandoning the boat, your first thought was for your own safety." "I protest! I protest!" I cry. "This is not true! The boys would agree the truth was that without me there was no hope of rescue from any source, my stupidity did get me into the situation, but my quick thinking was such that it saved them and avoided a major tragedy." The prosecuting counsel replied: "But you must be aware that the whaler turned over, the boys drowned like rats in a sewer, caught under the flat-bottomed barges by a racing tide. They had no chance." It was at this point I invariably awoke and thankfully my nightmare was replaced by reality.

As I write of this I realise I am engaged in a piece of therapy, something that should have been done twenty, thirty or forty years ago. I am writing this ghost out of my subconscious, a ghost that had haunted me with the tale of a tragedy that never was.

It is written that there is in the affairs of men a tide, which if taken at the flood leads onto fame and fortune, conversely, there is for exuberant youth, a tide that if taken on the ebb, leads out of peril to home and safety.

There was no tragedy, no heartbroken mothers to be faced, only a dangerous youthful episode that came close to a major scouting disaster. In the telling of it, I lay my ghost.

A Press Release

The purchase of two corvettes for the South African Navy produced a spate of pacifist correspondence in Cape Town.

Reflecting on my eighty years, some of it involved in British politics, I ask: how many times have I heard and in how many countries have I read the fine uplifting pacifist statement, (see Mr Crawford Browne, *The Argus*, February 24) and how many more times have these dangerous high-sounding sentiments led to disaster?

As a young man in London in 1936 with the Peace Pledge Union in full song I cheered the university debaters as they won the debate "that never again will they fight for King and country".

Men like the Rev Hewlett Johnson, the Red Dean of Canterbury, took my naiveté for a ride with many of my generation, as he found common ground between Karl Marx's *Das Kapital* and the Bible.

At the 1936 Fulham by-election we turned the conservative candidate's statement "with the rise of Hitler in Europe at least we should strengthen our defensive forces" into sounding like a vicious piece of war mongering.

The election posters showed fields of Flanders' poppies with the slogan that a vote for him would repeat 1914/18. It became a classic piece of electoral misrepresentation but it shattered a Tory majority to the dismay of the government.

No wonder Herr Ribbentrop convinced Hitler that Britain would never fight. History shows the truth that we could have stopped Hitler. He bluffed his way into the Saar with few guns, little ammunition and some tanks made of cardboard and orders to retreat if opposed. Nevertheless it was enough to frighten us. A half-duped generation, this was not hard to do.

By 1940 I had helped my neighbours in London Docklands leave their burning homes after the first German air raids on an open city. This was the moment of truth when, with so many others, we dustbinned our PPU badges and dumped Dr Hewlett Johnson and his 'Socialist Sixth of the World' into the refuse bin.

We were to learn the hard way that there are moments 'when it is better to die on your feet than to live on your knees'. Just how hard a lesson, the belated memorial to London's 40,000 dead will soon testify.

In modern times it seems unreal that the great Russian menace evaporated overnight – the Marxist dream of a land of plenty based on the nationalisation of all the means of production, distribution and exchange was after seventy years incapable of feeding its people let alone fighting a war.

The hopes of world peace have been short-lived. Not one nuclear threat but now a dozen.

The first euphoria, the short honeymoon, gives way to a new realism – the daily disclosures of ex-foreign government ministers, scientists, yesterday's generals, plus the Mafia scrambling to be the first with a modern nuclear device.

The possibility of Korea producing nuclear energy strikes fear through the middle and Far East.

We live in a dangerous world – a world that holds its breath for the future of this new nation and when one reads "that it is increasingly questionable whether South Africa needs an army, airforce or navy," this must be seen for the nonsense that it is.

The idea that South African frontiers can be secured with fields of daffodils and armies blowing kisses to an invader is in the spirit of the worst 'flower power' days of the seventies. It makes as much nonsense now as it did then.

Today my grandchild was born into this new nation. This is my tiny stake in immortality that will bind me into South Africa's future.

As I take my place in the queue at life's 'check out counter', to those who have yet to enter this pick and pay world let me quote this wise man's message:

> *Ill monda quam est viva –*
> We live in the world that we find.

> *Pro Monda quam viva Pugno –*
> We fight for the world that we want.

Victor E Waldron 17 March 1995
This article first appeared in the
Cape Town *Argus* 17/3/95

The Press, The Prince, The Present

Still too many
political leaders
give more obvious costs
of action than to
the concealed
costs of inaction.

HRH The Prince of Wales, 22/3/88

The Press is the biggest exponent of negativity in the modern world.

In twenty years, power hungry men have taken a medium of communication, once admired and trusted, and have created distrust and suspicion of which most men learn to be wary.

Many aspects of our lives are affected by politics in this area, a whole infantile vocabulary has been created – a change of mind always described as a "humiliating U-turn", a normal setback is a "slap in the face", a normal adjustment in policy as an "embarrassing cave-in" until the political scene seems to read like a comic strip.

Daily Telegraph, December 1994

Television and the tabloid press have replaced responsible journalism and the drift continues.

The Wall Street Journal wrote:

"The press sees its main function as making news, not reporting it. It has created a new journalism of sensationalism, a desire for scandal, controversy, excitement, titillation, and above all, the destruction of reputation."

Today, the newsman treats the truth of the evidence much like a dog uses a lamp post.

Today, the most negative reporting is reserved for the British Royal Family and the broken marriage of Prince Charles and Princess Diana.

Dimbleby's biography of 620 pages is judged on two extracts serialised by Rupert Murdoch in *The Sunday Times* before the book ever reached publication. This gave the world of the titillators a free run, leaving their interpretation unanswered. They competed in blacking the character of a Prince whose mistake was to marry for dynastic reasons a young girl who married her first love.

No fair-minded or dispassionate reader who reads the other five hundred pages would seek to attribute blame to either the Prince or Princess. This is a sad story, not a sex scandal. It tells of a Prince in search of a role for the monarchy in a modern world. An unhappy marriage is part of it. The story tells of the Princess' volatile behaviour, her resentment of his interests, her attempts to control his life, her jealousy. The book is not about a wimp but about a courageous and good man, his loneliness, his kindness, his stoicism, who continues to seek a place for the monarchy in the future world.

If the British people reject by referendum, membership of the European Union – which could well happen – and if the Labour Party's proposed partial self-government is granted to Wales and Scotland, England will then be on the way to becoming an off-shore island to the Union of Europe.

If that happens, the monarchy, which has been a power for unity and for good in English history, will have a new role to play. In Dimbleby's words "Less than ever can we afford the loss of the services of a Prince who is a wise, sensitive and intelligent and caring human being."

My Cousin, America

"Halt! Who goes there? Friend or foe?" The Beefeater Guard makes this challenge in a military exercise at the Tower of London and has done so every evening, without a break, since the days of the first Queen Elizabeth. The ceremony is a must on the itinerary of the American visitor and has been watched by thousands.

However quaint, this picture of historic England wallowing in its past is the impression I would like to alter.

The cynics claim that we are two nations separated by a common language. In a world full of uncertainty, to know who is your foe and who is your real friend is a need indeed.

I first experienced the unique quality of the American people as a newly promoted British Naval officer in my first action in the North African landing. I unexpectedly found myself under the command of the American General Dwight Eisenhower.

Here, I first met the American conviction expressed in war, and later in peace, that there was no problem, however difficult, however hard, however complicated, that you believed you could not handle, from going to the moon to making a fat-free cookie; everything was done with the sublime conviction that took one's breath away.

My concern is that, somewhere along the line, the confusion and uncertainty of my own country is being repeated, and this great quality of supreme confidence in your world destiny is deteriorating.

Is it a weakness, I ask, of the English-speaking people to occasionally lose sight of their own greatness? A common black out period, when we are no longer confident of our own magnificence? If this is so, if any seepage in your awareness to do great things is taking place, let's cry a 'halt' to that!

A handful of merchant venturers first took the English tongue, in Elizabeth's time, into the newly discovered world. In the next 350 years, wherever men met, wherever the humanities were understood, wherever the fundamental 'will to do good' (which is so much a part of the human spirit) was expressed, this was the language that was used.

I have stood at Lincoln's Memorial and read his words. I held my breath at the foot of the Statue of Liberty. The sheer, breathtaking achievement of taking the poor and hungry of our world and building a great nation in so short a time. Surely, then:

"God and some guiding star made you Americans what you are."

Too jingoistic, I hear you say. Not a thought for modern man. A little over the top, you think. Enough, then, of the past.

Lets talk of today. Every science, every medical breakthrough, every advance in communications, every electronic development, now and in the foreseeable future, depends, first and foremost, on the mastery of the English language – our common link. As a Brit, I have with you a vital interest and a special relationship that requires no ratified treaty to support it.

We are blood relatives, you and I. The blood of my father's generation mixed with yours, of this we are reminded annually by the blood-red fields of Flanders' poppies. Twenty years later, my generation was to turn to the New World once more, for succour and help in a common struggle in which we were close to exhaustion.

No other age in the history of mankind has had so much to offer the individual than the day and age in which we live. Yet we both make the common mistake of taking this so much for granted.

We live, cousin, in the world that we find. Together, we must fight for the world that we want.

Victor E. Waldron of Holmes Beach previously wrote a column for Manatee/AM Forum about his involvement in the Hunger Project.

IN PLACE OF AN EPILOGUE

Three poems by Gladys Echevarri Waldron 1913 – 1953

Two poems: an Indian Prayer and an Irish Blessing

Marriage
23rd April 1947

Is this the long-dreamed port of heart's desire?
Can here my soul's frail craft her anchor drop
And ride in quiet, the dreaming stars a-top?
These gentle waters, far from the red fire,
the smould'ring fire of sorrow? Can this bay
Of summer beauty, peace and loveliness
Sanctuary give from all the wild distress
She knew and weathered in that other day?

Or will the tempest enter even here
And tear this peace with its wild, ugly hands,
And hide the stars and darken all the sea,
And blind our eyes, and give our hearts to fear,
And drive my ship to other stranger lands
Where I shall seek and mourn and dream of thee?

William
born 25th September, 1948

Here is your son, I render back in him
The joy unspeakable which you have thrown
Around me like a cloak. For he has grown
In beauty, blossoming form out the grim
Shadows of patient pain, secret and sweet.
This loveliness, the living shape and form
Of the bright pulse of love. Here quite complete
The precious flowering of life's stress and storm.

O dear, my Love, a miracle is this.
More strange and wonderful than we could dream,
More rare than human heart would dare to pray.
Who could have guessed these tiny hands of his
Would hold within their grasp the blinding beam
Of God's perpetual, ever new-born Day?

October, 1948

Carola
born 3rd June 1953

Early Morning
3rd June 1953

"this is my offering to God
made possible through my
Dear husband and the reality
of our unity before God – and
a testing proof of our
partnership and love."

Gladys Echevarri Waldron died – 3rd June 1953

On Reaching Eighty

Indian Prayer (traditional)

When I am dead
Cry for me a little
Think of me sometimes
But not too much.
Think of me now and again
As I was in life
At some moments it's pleasant to recall
But not for long
Leave me in peace
And I shall leave you in peace
And while you live
Let your thoughts be with the living.

ANON

Dear Reader

May the road rise up
to meet you,
May the wind be always at your back,
May the sun shine warm
upon your face,
And the rains fall soft
upon your fields,
And until we meet again,
May God hold you
in the palm of his hand

An Irish Blessing